Effectively Efficient

Self-Care for Today's Fast-Paced World

NORBERT NIAKAS

Effectively Efficient: Self-Care for Today's Fast-Paced World
Copyright October 2024 by Norbert Niakas
All Rights Reserved.

No part of this book may be reproduced or transmitted in any form or by any means, electronic or mechanical, including photocopying, recording, or by any information storage or retrieval system without the written permission of the author, except where permitted by law.

Note: The information in this book is true and complete to the best the author's knowledge. As new information becomes available through research, experience, or changes to product contents, some of the data in this book may become invalid. This book is intended only as an informative guide to those wishing to know more about health issues. In no way is this book intended to replace, countermand, or conflict with the advice given to you by your own physician. The ultimate decision concerning care should be made between you and your doctor. The author strongly recommends you follow his or her advice. Information in this book is general and is offered with no guarantees on the part of the author. The author expressly disclaims responsibility for any adverse effects that may result from the application of the information contained in this book.

Mention of specific companies, organizations, or authorities in this book does not imply endorsement by the author, nor does mention of specific companies, organizations, or authorities imply that they endorse this book.

Author contact: Norbert.Niakas@gmail.com

To Mayuri and Anjali – Greatness awaits you!

Contents

Introduction vii

Chapter 1: The Path To Effectively Efficient Exercise. 1

Chapter 2: High-Intensity Training 13

Chapter 3: Transition of HIT & HIIT to the Home. 29

Chapter 4: Health Benefits of Exercise 43

Chapter 5: Building Motivation To Exercise 57

Chapter 6: One Man's Food Journey 75

Chapter 7: Nutrition Concensus. 85

Chapter 8: Fasting. 105

Chapter 9: Goal Setting 119

Chapter 10: Meditation 137

Chapter 11: Conclusion. 155

Appendix: The Self Experiment 161

References. 187

Introduction

Twenty-Four

This number may conjure up different thoughts for different people, such as the title of a popular television series, famous Hall of Fame baseball player Ken Griffey Jr.'s jersey number, the age you were when you had the energy to stay out all night, or the birthdate of your favorite relative. Most likely though, we quickly connect this number to the number of hours in a day.

24 hours.

The origin of the 24-hour day dates back to the ancient Egyptians and their use of sun dials and water clocks. In modern American times, we've enhanced our methods for time-telling, and have also mastered how to fill the 24 hours allotted to us each day. We Americans are busy people. In fact, in a 2018 survey conducted by the Pew Research Center, 60% of adults responded that they are sometimes too busy to enjoy life. The eight bullet point sequence below takes us from 24 hours to zero in less than 60 seconds. From the totality of a Monday through Friday, subtract the following:

- Between seven and eight hours for generally deemed optimal sleep, as 65 percent of the United States population reports sleeping this amount (Liu et al. 2016).

- Between five (remote) and eight (workplace) hours for work (Bureau of Labor Statistics 2023). Per 2023 statistics, only 12.2 percent of Americans work fully remote (Carpenter 2024).

- Fifty minutes to one hour for each day commuting to work (United States Census Bureau 2022).

- 30 minutes to one hour in the bathroom (believe me on this one, or time yourself tomorrow)

- One hour for eating and drinking; interestingly people living in the United States spend the least time eating and drinking compared to populations of over 20 other developed nations (Ortiz-Ospina et al. 2024).

- Two hours for housework and shopping (Ortiz-Ospina et al. 2024).

- One more hour If you have children between 6 and 17; two hours if they are under 6 (Bureau of Labor Statistics 2023).

- The remaining hours will likely be spent watching TV (cable, broadcast, and TV connected devices), considering the average adult spends almost 5 hours a day doing so (Marketing Charts 2023).

Something important is missing in this weekday outline: time for self-care. Although our focus here is on weekdays, weekends provide opportunity for self-care as well, but these two days tend to be less structured for most of us. Weekends are also used predominantly for more sleeping, leisure, and housework (Vo 2012). Hence, let's stick with the weekdays and narrow self-care down to three specific types because they are the main topics of this book – exercise, healthy eating, and meditation. There is extensive evidence that these three, if incorporated regularly, can greatly enhance health. Yet, how much time do we need for each?

The Centers for Disease Control and Prevention (CDC) recommends 150 minutes of moderate intensity physical activity a week plus two days out of the week during which one performs muscle-strengthening activities. Exercising during the weekdays, which may lead to successfully continuing the behavior due to the built-in structure of these days, requires 30 minutes a day of some sort of "aerobic" activity and likely another 45 minutes two of the five days for resistance training. Per the United States Department of Health and Human Services (2018), around one in four Americans meet these physical activity guidelines. And that's just exercise. What about healthy eating?

For now, let's focus on only one aspect of healthy eating – cooking. Although far from nutritionally full proof, cooking at home at the least provides the opportunity to control one's ingredients, unlike when one eats out. How much time do we need for cooking? While the amount of time varies based on age, sex, and socioeconomic status, a fair estimate is somewhere between 37 and 53 minutes for meal prep, cooking, and cleaning per day (Hamrick 2016; US Bureau of Labor Statistics 2023). Prepping healthy meals may take longer. No wonder most Americans eat fast food at least once a week (Rodgers 2023), whether that's via drive-through, at a restaurant, or better yet pay a bit extra for delivery, relax on the couch, and eat while catching up on TV time.

What about meditation, or any other form of mindfulness practice? This recommendation varies greatly, usually starting out as low as five minutes (Lam et al. 2015) to 45 minutes per day (Khoury et al. 2015), and beyond. Exercise, nutrition, and meditation all require consistency to attain health benefits. Overall, if we add up the time we should spend exercising, cooking, and meditating, we are likely looking at anywhere from one and a half to two hours per weekday. Take a quick peak back at the 24-hour weekday breakdown on the prior page and consider where this time is going to go. The time crunch is significant, especially for working and commuting parents. Are these self-care recommendations realistic if you have a full-time commuter job, children, and other unavoidable responsibilities? Can you, and more importantly, do you want to shift a chunk of the self-care time to the weekends? Is that shift beneficial considering daily consistency is important with self-care? For those who have ample free time, are you motivated to use it on these strategies versus relaxing, decompressing, and enjoying other comfortable activities? I propose that all three of these impactful forms of self-care can be incorporated in significantly less time than the averages and recommendations, while providing amazing results and health benefits. I'm also hopeful that the content in this book will inspire those who have the time but are still in the contemplation phase of incorporating these forms of self-care.

America's Health Plight

Why do these self-care strategies matter? Within the hustle and bustle of the average American adult's life, going from one place to the next, often on the run, burning through the day's hours at a frantic pace, the profoundly balancing reality is that in this rat race, we barely need to move physically. Per CDC statistics, Americans are seated for six and a half to eight hours each day (Barrell 2023), while working, driving, eating, talking, internet shopping, ordering food, scrolling, and contemplating exercise. We lay on our backs another seven to eight hours sleeping, or attempting to sleep, and are likely in some sort of reclined in-between state of leisure watching a small or large screen for another four to five hours per day. The endless array of ways to enhance the opportunity not to move does not align with most of mankind's existence on this planet, that being a need for movement. This stationary state is further exacerbated by the questionable, processed food-like substances available for our consumption, the intake of which is connected to the obesity epidemic and poor health outcomes for many Americans (Masood & Moorthy 2023; Poti et al. 2017). The mental health crisis further compounds these health outcomes. Bottom line, we are not well due to various reasons, and the outlook for trend reversal is rather bleak.

Considering the concerning state of health in this country, with a continued tendency towards movement-negating comfort, mindless scrolling, and the overabundance and marketing of ultra processed food, plus a medical system that is more reactive than preventative, efforts to incorporate self-care are pivotal in reversing the current health trends. Each one of us needs to take ownership of our health and overall well-being. But as outlined earlier, self-care takes time. Or does it? Is it possible to minimize the amount of time we spend on self-care in the form of exercise, healthy eating, and mindfulness, while still attaining significant benefits from these activities? What if effective exercise, healthy eating, and mental health self-care could all be accomplished in 10 to 15 minutes each, per day – or even less? One of the main reasons that Americans provide for not living a healthier lifestyle is a lack of time to do so. What if we could address the "I don't have time" response and create high quality, structured self-care while building motivation to perform these behaviors?

The Goods and The Sell

The information in this book is not rocket science nor is it a groundbreaking new finding. They are concepts, ideas, and systems that have been around for a while. At some point though, for one reason or another, they fell out of favor, were forgotten, or simply deserve further expounding on. In a country where the drive for newer and bigger and better is powerful, sometimes a return to simpler, with a focus on effectiveness, is a necessary pivot. I'm hopeful that my unique perspective, stories, and experience sparks interest, intrigue, inspiration – and most importantly, action!

And who am I? A working man, husband, and father of two who at several points in his life felt the crunch of the 24-hour day, but who was unwilling to allow the ever-changing flow of life and new responsibilities to negatively impact the quality of his self-care. As I aged and responsibilities grew, I saw an opportunity to re-assess, adjust, and continue to move forward. In addition to sharing my story, process, and personal insight, this book includes stories about subject matter experts within the realm of health, as well as impactful accounts of change from everyday people I've met during my life journey. As a professional, I've served others in the capacity of a personal trainer, health coach, life skills counselor, case manager, probation officer, trainer, lecturer, interviewer, mentor, and presenter. The responsibility that came with these roles provided me with deeper insight into accountability, motivation, support, respect, empathy, struggle, trauma, passion, and purpose. I know that my responsibility on this planet is to serve others and this book is an extension of that service.

For those of you reading this who spend plenty of time in your day on self-care strategies, I ask – why not shorten that time significantly and create more time for other things you enjoy? Instead of spending hours in the gym and meal prepping each week, wouldn't it be better to spend less time on those activities and more time focusing on different projects of passion, pursuits, and other forms of personal growth? Or just spend more time with family and friends, have fun, and travel. Considering some of the benefits of exercise include improved mental health, mood, physical fitness, health span, quality of life, and prevention of numerous diseases (Ruegsegger & Booth 2018; Mahindru et al. 2023), why not spend as much time as possible enjoying these benefits versus attaining them? Of course, there is a social bonding factor to the gym life which I've personally experienced and cannot deny, yet having an alternative training system that does not require extensive time, especially for days that we just want to get the training over with, holds great value. Furthermore, the exercise philosophy described in this book is perfect for home workouts, a space that may be more difficult in which to get motivated to train.

The Content

In the first few chapters, we rediscover an exercise philosophy that is the most efficient, effective, and safe – high-intensity training, with a secondary focus on high-intensity interval training. You'll learn about the benefits of exercise, whether it is effective for weight loss, and the importance of building and maintaining muscle into our golden years – for both women and men. If you have eclipsed the age of 40, like myself, and have yet to incorporate resistance training in your life, I hope that these chapters spark the motivation to do so immediately!

Next, we'll focus on building motivation to exercise. Considering exercise should be a life-long undertaking, it's essential to understand motivation and incorporate long-term motivational strategies for this all-important behavior.

Following motivation, we'll explore the United States food system and assess the aspects of nutrition and diet agreed on by subject matter experts. We'll also take a deep dive into the issues with sugar and simple/refined carbohydrate consumption, processed food, learn about several healthy home cooked meals that can be prepped and enjoyed quickly, and address intermittent/time-restricted fasting.

We'll then move to the topic of goals as I share my personal experience with goal setting and how this process has significantly altered my career and life paths – for the better. I'll provide insight into proven goal setting strategies and some examples of their successful implementation.

The next section focuses on meditation through insight into this game-changing practice, both from a personal and evidence-based perspective. I'll also share the story of a chi-gung master, which displays the boundless power of meditation and proper breathing.

Lastly, In the appendix, I provide an in-depth look into a dietary self-experiment which lasted several months and included the reincorporation of poultry and beef into my diet after 13 years of being either vegetarian or pescatarian, among other dietary changes. The purpose of the experiment was to see if I could burn fat while maintaining muscle in my mid-40s with simple and efficient dietary interventions. What happened? Check out the appendix!

Effectively Efficient

The words effective and efficient are sometimes used together, separated by "and". What do these words mean individually?

> *Effective – successful in producing a desired or intended result.*
> *Efficient – achieving maximum productivity*
> *with minimum wasted effort.*

Now let's combine them – "Effectively Efficient." What does it mean to be effectively efficient with our self-care? It means that we are succeeding in producing desired results and attaining benefits from the behavior in the shortest time possible, with minimum to zero wasted effort. My main goal in writing this book is to provide options for self-care that can be accomplished in little time, with big results. I want you to get the most out of the time you spend on yourself. How ambitious can we be with this process? Read on and find out!

The term effectively efficient is not reserved for self-care only, but also how one functions every day. For me, it means being the best version of myself so that I can navigate each day with confidence, clarity, and smoothly adapt to the everchanging dynamics of life. Furthermore, when we are at our best, physically and mentally, the people around us get the best version of us. We can mitigate a stressful situation at work in the morning, deal with an annoying co-worker in the afternoon, sit at peace in unexpected traffic on our way home, and still have the energy to play with our kids, give some time to our partner, wash dishes, and maybe work on our personal passion of choice in the evening. An alternative narrative with no daily self-care may include emotionally eating something unhealthy after the stressful morning, getting in an argument with our annoying co-worker in the afternoon, cussing up a storm in the unexpected traffic, and ending our day prematurely by passing out on the couch in front of the television while our unsupervised kids draw an expansive crayon mosaic on the wall, and our annoyed partner single-handedly tackles the cooking and cleaning. I prefer the first scenario for both you and me.

I sincerely thank you and appreciate you for opening this book. Whether you are a 46-year-old working father and husband (like me), a 25-year-old single fitness buff who exercises three hours a day, a 65-year-old retiree who enjoys reading mystery novels over an evening cup of chamomile tea, or a 36-year-old mother of four who is simply trying to survive each day, I'm confident there is something in this book for you. Most importantly, if you are someone who wants to spend as little time as possible on exercise, nutrition, and mindfulness so that you can create more time for your passions and to spend with the people you love, and be at your best every day, the information in this book is absolutely for you! There is one important health-related factor that will not be directly addressed in this book – sleep. Sleeping less than seven hours per night is associated with diabetes, coronary heart disease, stroke, and all-cause mortality (Liu et al. 2016). Quality sleep is necessary if we want to feel great every day, and thankfully the self-care strategies discussed in this book are all linked to better sleep (Alnawwar et al. 2023; Black et al. 2015; Godos et al. 2021).

Now without further ado, it's time for you to learn how to become effectively efficient with your self-care so that you can be effectively efficient in all that you do!

Chapter 1

The Path To Effectively Efficient Exercise

A Champion's Story

Bob Backlund had a difficult upbringing. He grew up in a small farming community in Minnesota where his family made ends meet to the best of their ability. To compound the social-economic issues, Bob's father had a drinking problem. The unpredictability of his father's drunken states and abuse made Bob's life extremely difficult and the home a place that he tried to avoid. School was an outlet, but unfortunately Bob struggled there with both his studies and socialization. He didn't have many friends or much support. Attempts to get involved in after-school sports didn't work out well either as Bob was unathletic and uncoordinated. As with many youths who experience trauma in the home and struggle at school, Bob fell in with the wrong crowd by 6th-grade. He started hanging out with older kids and getting into fights regularly. One specific event, which placed his life in danger, was the final realization that he was headed down a dead-end path (Backlund & Miller 2015).

Bob revisited sports in the 8th-grade, specifically football and wrestling. Although he was still not very good at athletics, Bob stuck with sports even as he continued to struggle with schoolwork. His sophomore year of high school was a turning point in his personal growth and progression. Bob watched another high school sophomore win the local wrestling finals and something clicked. That teenager became his role model as Bob realized that he wanted to accomplish the same success. Soon after, he was introduced to weight training. Bob took to the weights quickly and fervently, and with results came motivation. As part of his training to strengthen his neck, he attached a 25-pound barbell plate to an old football helmet and went for long runs with the helmet on. Since he was not a natural athlete, Bob realized there was another path towards athletic success – outworking everyone else. The impact of this realization shifted Bob's life in a positive direction, and he ultimately became a NCAA and professional wrestling champion (Backlund & Miller 2015).

Athletics In Youth and Grit

The importance of athletics and/or some other form of consistent activities in childhood cannot be understated. In her book, *Grit: The Power of Passion and Perseverance*, MacArthur Fellow winner and psychology professor Angela Duckworth expounded on the positive impact of children being challenged through sports or other skill-based activities. Sticking with the activity and persisting even though things may become difficult is a key as well. Coaches are there to correct, push, and support this process. The result can be the development of grit for the youth, which can serve the athletic or activity success at that time and become engrained as a permanent trait. Considering that grit can be a bigger marker for success than IQ, the development of this trait holds great value.

In his autobiography, *Backlund: From All-American Boy to Professional Wrestling's World Champion*, Bob noted the importance of involving kids in athletics, which is also one of his Eighteen Principles of Healthy Living:

> Find a way to get your kids involved in athletics from a young age. Doing so will teach them discipline, responsibility, and how to be part of a team. It will give them strength and balance and build their concentration and self-esteem. (p. 476)

Bob's advice is backed up by Duckworth's extensive research. Although Bob did not specifically mention grit, it's clear that athletics and understanding the importance and benefits of hard work were his vehicle to developing this importance trait. Athletics are typically the first purposeful physical activity that children are introduced to. Prior to that, it's just a lot of uninhibited, carefree running around, something we are all wired for because the human body is meant to move. Unfortunately, as kids enter school age, the dynamics of the classroom set-up and unrealistic expectation of sedentary learning for extensive hours begins to negatively impact the body and need for movement. Television, video games, and other forms of effortless entertainment do further damage. At this point in the youth's life, along with tapping into grit, athletics and other regular physical activity can serve as an outlet for the natural need to move.

As mentioned prior, Bob's athletic path served as a vehicle for weight training. One of the other major benefits of athletics is youth developing the understanding that physical exercise greatly enhances their chances for success in their sport of choice. Upon that realization, depending on their commitment, the opportunity presents itself to incorporate specific physical training into their lives. In Bob's case, the positive feedback that his body provided from the weight training, specifically enhancement of strength and muscle, further pushed his efforts in wrestling and football. Positivity fed positivity in a wonderful circle of reinforcement, which bolstered his motivation. In his case and for most kids involved in sports, exercise becomes the second purposeful physical activity that they are introduced to.

The Importance of Movement

If you want to be effectively efficient, movement, and more importantly purposeful movement that will enhance health, is non-negotiable. Which means that a predominantly sedentary lifestyle without physical effort is not an option. Unfortunately, just like with food, which we will unpack later, our societal structure in the United States has made convenience and comfort, with little need for regular movement, our functional defaults. It takes little to no effort to develop a sedentary lifestyle while movement has become an effortful and mindful endeavor. Combining a lack of purposeful movement with the Standard American Diet (SAD) heavy in sugar, processed foods, and refined carbohydrates, creates a path towards obesity and associated diseases. Those diseases, which include diabetes and heart disease, influence the United States' inferior health outcomes and shorter lifespans when compared to other high-income countries (National Research Council 2013). The poor health outcomes factor into one of the costliest health care systems in the world. Outside of the larger scale impact of lifestyle-related diseases, there are the negative effects experienced by every person who suffers from these diseases, with consequences for their immediate family.

The human body always required some level of movement, guided by the basic need for survival and ultimately, reproduction. Hunter gatherers utilized energy, whether that was via quick bursts, long walks, digging, or throwing, to attain energy in the form of food out of necessity. Since those times, which make up most of human existence on this planet, our biology has not adjusted for movement to become obsolete. Thankfully, the options for regular, purposeful movement in the form of exercise are plentiful as humans have developed countless ways to challenge their bodies in the face of sedentary living. Yet not all these systems and philosophies are equally effective. A usual recommendation when one contemplates starting exercise, which makes sense, is to engage in physical activities that one likes. There is an alternative path though, which we'll embark on shortly. First, let's return to the legendary professional and collegiate wrestling champion, Bob Backlund.

Interview with Bob

Through a combination of goal setting, universal intervention, a cold email, and perseverance, in 2019 I landed an in-person interview with Bob. My buddy Will and I arrived in Connecticut on a pleasant, sunny April weekday and met Bob at a local library. We quickly assessed that the space in the library would not be adequate to conduct the interview and Bob was kind enough to recommend his home gym as an alternative. In hindsight, I think that may have been his plan all along, but he probably wanted to feel us out first in a neutral space, which I don't blame him for. Two random guys driving up from Jersey are worthy of a deeper character assessment. Bob probably wanted to size us up as well, and I am not ashamed to say that he could easily manhandle my friend and me by himself at the age of 69. Bob was well known for his strength and catch wrestling skills, which he still possessed. I had the pleasure of getting stretched out a bit by Bob later in the day, and by stretched out I don't mean in a therapeutic manner.

Bob's home gym was covered in memorabilia, including the tournament brackets from his scholastic wrestling championships on the walls. As we set up the camera and two seats for the interview shoot, Bob mentioned that he avoids sitting and prefers to either stand or lay down almost all the time. Since conducting the interview laying down would likely raise some eyebrows of prospective YouTube viewers, we went with the standing option. There is plenty of science to back Bob's concerns with sitting, as our bodies are not designed for this purpose. In his book, *Deskbound: Standing Up to a Sitting World*, Kelly Starrett took a deep dive into the plethora of physical issues caused by consistent sitting. Some of these include the forward head posture in the cervical spine which can cause neck pain, tightness in the upper back, and headaches; further issues include reduced hip flexion, shortened hamstrings, and elongated, inactive and weak glutes. The longer we remain sitting, the greater the chance that we default into a bad position as it is not possible to sit for an extended amount of time and keep the back properly supported. If you must sit regularly, Starrett's suggestions included sitting upright on the edge of the chair, so your weight is distributed over the bony parts of your pelvis. If you sit back in the chair, your weight is distributed to your glutes and hamstrings which are not designed to be weight-bearing surfaces. Get up every 20 to 25 minutes to walk around and/or stretch before sitting down again.

We began the interview, and I asked several prepared questions, which Bob surprisingly answered in full wrestling character mode. We next transitioned to a 30-minute ad-libbed interview and exercise demonstrations. The non-scripted, free flowing exchanges worked beautifully, starting with me being painfully stretched out via a circular alternating seated straddle stretch. This was followed by Bob embarrassing me during a standing touch-your-toes stretch when he placed his palms fully on the ground while I managed to barely nip the floor with my fingertips. Next, I joined Bob in a demonstration of isometrics, an underutilized yet impactful exercise system. Isometric exercises involve the tightening of muscle groups for a specific amount of time for the purpose of strength building and maintenance. One of the main benefits of isometrics is that the exercises can be done anywhere and anytime without any equipment. Bob and I focused on tightening our biceps and glutes, followed by a transition to more stretching.

The two exercises that Bob introduced next are the bread and butter of his workout program, and a segway into the bread and butter of this chapter. When Bob traveled during his time as a professional wrestler in the 70s and 80s, it was not always easy to locate a gym in the immediate area of where the wrestling show was. This led to him creating a two-exercise training program, one for the lower body and one for the upper body. The first exercise was an extension of the Harvard step test, which involves stepping on and off a 12-inch block or the equivalent of a stair step. The original test was designed to measure a participant's aerobic fitness and lasted three minutes. Bob extended the timeframe to one hour for his purposes, which is A LOT of steps. Considering that professional wrestling is an extremely physical sport, Bob was the world champion for a long time, and fit, muscular physiques were and still are an expectation in pro wrestling, it makes perfect sense that Bob needed to train extensively. The Harvard step test, when extended past it's "testing" time into an endurance exercise, strengthens the major muscles of the lower body and provides cardiovascular benefits.

Bob's second exercise utilized one of the few gimmicky, muscle group targeting equipment that works, the Ab Wheel. Developed in the 1960s with the promise of great abs in short time, the Ab Wheel has stuck around as an abdominal exercise option for over sixty years. But how could Bob strengthen much of his upper body with an exercise devised to only target the abs? Bob adjusted the exercise to make it as effective as possible in targeting other upper body muscle groups and performed it an average of 400 repetitions per exercise session. Again, for a professional athlete who does not have access to a gym, this is fair game. Let's walk through Bob's process of targeting muscle groups other than the abdominals via the Ab Wheel.

A Different Spin on the Ab Wheel

The classic method of Ab Wheel utilization involves, from a knees-on-the-ground position, rolling the wheel out until the upper body is close to full if not fully extended, and then rolling the wheel back towards the knees to the starting position. This constitutes one repetition. Bob's version had one major tweak which changed the dynamic of the entire exercise. When fully extended, instead of raising the hips up before returning the wheel to its starting position, Bob rolled the wheel back under his chest first, which activated the muscle groups of the upper body, and then raised his hips to return the wheel back to the starting position. This makes the exercise more difficult. To increase the impact of the exercise further, Bob squeezed the handles of the wheel during the return portion of the exercise. During our interview and exercise demonstration, I initially performed this Ab Wheel variation incorrectly. When Bob corrected my form to his version, I felt the difference of the exercise immediately, specifically via the activation of my triceps and lats. To this day I still use this devise, but only Bob's version, specifically when I exercise my triceps. Overall, the Ab Wheel holds value even if targeting the abdominals only.

The Need to Become Effectively Efficient with Exercise

Bob's step test and wheel exercise routine takes an hour and a half to complete and is very effective as a full body workout which provided Bob with strength, fitness, and cardiovascular benefits of an elite athlete. It has kept him fit and functional into his 70s. I adopted the wheel portion of his system because it fit within the guidelines of my effective and efficient exercise process, although not at the amount of time and repetitions that Bob used since my fitness goals do not fall within the realm of world wrestling champion and elite athlete. I cannot overstate the importance of setting very specific goals for what we want to look like, feel like, and function like to ensure that whatever exercise system we choose to incorporate is ideal for our purposes. Also, considering he wrestled in small wrestling trunks in front of thousands of people every night, along with the physical demands, Bob's exercise regimen fit that reality. Considering I teach and train employees every few weeks, fully clothed every single time, I have set my exercise standards based on that reality. Don't get me wrong though, if I did my job shirtless, I'm confident no one would be upset.

I initially arrived at my current rate of 10 minute-a-day workouts, which includes time for breaks within those 10 minutes, out of necessity, not choice. When I began weight training at the age of 19 and all the way to age 36, I had plenty of time to exercise daily. In line with this timeframe, per recent data, the age demographic that goes to the gym the most is the 18 to 34 group (Smith 2023), likely because they have the time. During these years, I visited the gym five to six days a week, spending anywhere from 40 minutes to an hour training each day. Normally, the workout would be dedicated to high-volume resistance training, with a focus on one muscle group a day. Aerobic-specific exercises such as running on the treadmill or using the stationary bike would be randomly sprinkled in. The time spent in the gym was reinforced by always having one or multiple training partners, which enhanced motivation. The impact of a dependable workout partner cannot be understated. For some who I know, a workout partner is a necessary motivational driver to even make it into the gym in the first place.

At age 36, my first daughter, Mayuri, arrived. For those of you who had an established training routine and then became a parent, you may be able to relate to the reality of new responsibilities impacting old routines. I was also holding down a full-time job, a part-time job, and working on side projects when she was born. The six days a week of driving to the gym was no longer feasible and I needed to adjust. My wife understood the importance of exercise in my life and was ok with me still going to the gym, although not at the same rate as before. I cut the gym to three-to-four days a week and maxed out my time at 40 minutes per training session, on average. I had to speed up the workouts, curb the socialization, and incorporate two body part-a-day routines. This worked fine to maintain my established fitness level. I also incorporated some at-home workouts to supplement what I was doing in the gym, although building motivation to exercise at home was difficult.

Two and a half years later, my second daughter, Anjali, was born, which further increased my home and parenting responsibilities. I still worked both full and part-time to support my family. The gym visits dwindled to two days a week on average during which time I still aimed to target two body parts through high-volume resistance training. The home workouts increased slightly. Aerobic exercise was nonexistent (luckily, it's far from a necessity, which I learned years later). Without my gym partners, I still lacked the motivation to exercise at home regularly. With this exercise time crunch I needed to figure something out quickly because not training adequately, and up to my standards, was not an option.

Discovering an Old Training System

I'm a firm believer that things happen for a reason, quite often. Maybe all the time but we only recognize it if we really tune in. I don't remember the exact circumstance of how I stumbled upon Doug McGuff's and John Little's *Body by Science,* but it was clearly for a reason and was the perfect antidote for my exercise situation at that time. Approximately four months after the birth of Anjali, I began reading the book that completely altered my understanding of exercise. Before we take a deep dive into the training philosophy that changed my life and spurred the need to share my exercise story, we must first discuss the impact of Arthur Jones.

Body by Science introduced me to Jones, but Ellington Darden's *The New High-intensity Training* provided a deeper understanding of this fascinating human being. Since our focus here is on exercise, we'll stick to what Jones accomplished within the realm of the body-building world, with the main contribution being his invention of Nautilus training machines and utilization of high-intensity training. To this day, the mechanism of the machines, no matter how archaic they may seem, is perfectly designed for a continued state of resistance from top to bottom of a repetition. Jones understood that "...muscles had different levels of strength throughout their range of motion" (McGuff & Little, 2009, p. 68). Learning more about Jones and his work provided me with an appreciation for exercise machines. For most of my exercising life and work as a personal trainer, body weight exercises and free weights were the preferred options and what I recommended to clients. Both are highly effective ways to train but now I also understood the impact of machines for muscle growth and maintenance.

I also developed a deeper level of appreciation for exercise intensity and recovery. Jones was a master of pushing his competitive body builders through extremely intense training routines on the machines, but also figured out that once one taps into high-intensity, longer recovery is required for optimal muscle growth. With two young kids, a full and part-time job, and other familial responsibilities, the high-intensity training system was exactly what I needed considering the necessity to get the most out of my limited time for exercise. It also required one very important mental shift which Jones captured in the following quote: "If you like doing barbell curls, chances are you are doing them wrong" (Darden 2004, p. 6).

As mentioned earlier, the usual recommendation for starting an exercise/movement program of any sort is to find something you like to do. This makes sense as we are more likely to continue doing something that we enjoy and have fun doing. Maybe it's a nice, daily walk in the park, a recreational sport, jogging, etc. This is great for incorporating movement into one's life and enjoying the benefits of low to moderate intensity activities. Humans have been walking on this planet for a very long time and the benefits of this very basic movement are plentiful. Yet, these types of low impact activities tend to be time consuming and do not provide the same level of muscle growth as high-intensity training. Therefore, they are not efficient while also not maximizing effectiveness. These activities should not be deemed as exercise. This brings us back to goals. Is your goal to get off the couch and simply start doing something? Is it to move more? To what extent will movement that is fun, pleasant, and relatively easy enhance your health? How much time are you willing to devote towards these activities and are they challenging enough to sustain motivation? Or maybe you're willing to up the intensity, shorten the time, and enjoy more benefits?

My interpretation of Jones' quote and the mentality with which I've incorporated high-intensity training into my life, is that exercise is not supposed to be a very pleasant experience, if performed correctly. I don't look forward to high-intensity training as I am not a masochist at heart. The beauty of it is that the discomfort is brief, with excellent health-related returns. The cover of *Body by Science* states, "A research-based program for strength training, body building, and complete fitness in 12 minutes a week." This is probably hard to believe but accurate if the exercises and level of intensity purported are incorporated properly. There are also fascinating psychological benefits to high-intensity training that we will discuss later.

Muscle Is King

High-intensity training, as introduced in the prior segment, is a resistance training system. The goal is to build muscle. Muscle is the fountain of youth. All Ponce De Leon had to do was research the history of resistance training in Ancient Greece and incorporate what they did instead of the risky proposition of a boat trip to Florida in the 1500s. The benefits of maintaining muscle mass cannot be understated, especially as we age. Research shows that senior citizens with the least muscle mass are at the greatest risk of dying from all causes (Attia 2023). Resistance training increases bone density, which in turn reduces the risk of osteoporosis. If you fall at an age where falls can be debilitating due to fractures, stronger muscle and bones will reduce the chance of that worst case scenario. Muscle on our body also speeds up metabolism as there is a greater energetic cost due to its presence alone. It improves general functionality, with increased mobility and flexibility. It can also increase coordination and of course, it makes us look better and more desirable, which can boost self-confidence.

Resistance training has been historically an exercise system used by men, which is a problematic trend that needed to end yesterday. Muscle benefits everyone. Resistance training is equally important and beneficial for women and women should perform it the same way men do, via free weights, their bodies, and machines. Unfortunately, the fitness industry has created differentiation between how men and women should exercise, where gimmicky training programs for women take place of direct and effective muscle building strategies. Part of this is due to the unrealistic fear of women becoming too bulky or muscular if they resistance train like men. This is highly unlikely to happen. High-intensity training holds benefits for both men and women. I've seen it firsthand when I personal trained female clients using the high-intensity principles discussed in the next chapter.

Chapter 2

High-Intensity Training

Hit It!

Before I continue with my story and the benefits I've experienced through high-intensity training, take a few minutes to reflect on the following questions: What is your physical activity or exercise level right now? What are you doing regularly to optimize your fitness? How much time do you spend each week exercising? Would you like to attain similar if not greater fitness and health benefits in significantly less time? What holds more value for you: spending more time doing something that is less physically challenging or less time doing something that is very challenging? Would you like to build muscle and reap the health benefits of it in the least amount of time possible? Should physical activity or exercise take so much time that you may not be able to allot necessary hours towards other projects? Or should exercise be a vehicle not only to create those extra hours but make you as effective as possible while you utilize them? Why not enjoy more time using the healthy body and accompanying energy you've attained through exercise.

The incorporation of high-intensity training has not only optimized my fitness and overall health, but it has also reframed the purpose of exercise in my life. Before, I viewed exercise as an activity in itself, with a clear understanding that it made me look and feel better. This made sense and the results still hold value to this day. My current enhanced view of exercise is the following: very brief exercise is a tool that enhances how I function every day and creates more time to spend on other activities, projects, etc. while still looking and feeling good. It has become a strategy for being my best or close to every day.

After I read *Body by Science,* I incorporated the exercise concepts from the book into my gym workouts, with the goal of assessing how little exercise at high-intensity I could perform each week. I started this process by cutting my gym days to once a week (I only had two free days anyway) and targeted the major muscle groups as recommended in the book, using machines only. I wanted to see if the results of my high-volume workout routines of yesteryears could be had with minimal, high-intensity training. Before we get to the outcome, let's differentiate high-volume training from high-intensity training.

High-Volume vs. High-Intensity

My old way of training under the high-volume principles, although effective for building muscle and strength, was not efficient due to the amount of time I spent in the gym. My high-volume routine usually involved several sets consisting of a specific number of reps, and numerous exercises for the same muscle group. For example, a chest day may consist of bench press, four sets of 10 reps, butterflies at three sets for 10 reps, incline bench press at three sets for 10 reps, and maybe decline dumbbell presses at three sets for 10 reps. That was A LOT of stimulation for the chest muscles and very time consuming. Yet, this was the path most who resistance trained in the gym took. Each repetition was usually one to two seconds concentric (positive), and one to two seconds eccentric (negative) – my training partners and I were "banging out sets." Did I really need to spend that much time on sets and repetitions every single workout? Could I have been overtraining and possibly built even more muscle through more intense but less frequent training? Even if I had only performed one exercise per body part at a rate of three set for 10 reps, that still fell within the realm of high volume and then became highly dependent on the weight used, time of breaks between sets, and whether the last reps were close to muscle failure, to determine positive effects.

The goal of resistance training is to build muscle and strength, and high-intensity training (HIT) is a very direct path to that end. As stated earlier, building and maintaining muscle is essential to a healthy and functional life into old age. Through HIT, the trainee recruits all the targeted muscle fibers by going to muscular failure using challenging weight, which stimulates growth and strength, with adequate rest after each workout (McGuff & Little 2009). This is usually accomplished with a one set effort, versus being broken down into sets with rest time in between. With high-volume training, the trainee performs one set of a specific number of reps, and then takes a break. During that break, some of the muscle fibers may recover before the second set is attempted. After the second set, the same thing may happen again. By the end of the three or four sets, the trainee likely did not fatigue all muscle fibers adequately because of the breaks in-between, therefore not getting the most out of their workout.

If you currently utilize sets and reps for your resistance training, try this the next time you go to the gym or train at home: track your time under load, meaning the actual amount of time that you are lifting the weights during each set. Then add the combined time for all the sets. How long did you work for? Was it at least a minute for the several sets? Consider that the time under load for a high-intensity set is preferably 90 seconds, not exceeding two minutes. The reality is that one high-intensity set may provide the opportunity to perform more actual work than several sets of high-volume training (HVT).

I trained high-volume for over 15 years because it worked to build muscle, no one showed me other options, nor did I discover any on my own during that time. Even though my training partners and I sometimes used negatives, static holds, and slowed down our repetitions, we always returned to what we knew best and were most comfortable with. We also firmly believed that the more lifting we did, the better. Further reinforcement came from muscle magazines which generally supported high-volume training. Everyone in the gym lifted weights this way. I have not worked out in a gym since early 2020 but I assume high-volume training, or some new fast-paced exercise formats are the current status quo. So, which is better for results, HIT or HVT? Hass at el. (2000) found that increasing the training volume for recreational weightlifters after an initial year of minimal dose resistance training did not result in any greater fitness improvements than if these weightlifters continued with the minimal dose. Furthermore, a 2016 study found that both HIT and HVT can result in significant muscular performance gains, but the muscular performance gains from HIT may be greater (Giessing et al.). It's important to note that in this study, the HIT trainees exercised an average of 10.5 minutes while the HVT group exercised between 24 and 27 minutes per session. My personal experience and preference: I'll take HIT every time as I've attained the same if not better results in significantly less time spent exercising.

A Shift In Mentality

For the years that I exercised under the resistance training high-volume principles, I was locked into the set and rep mindset. This is common for most individuals who resistance train in a gym. One locks into a certain number of sets, usually around three or four for a specific exercise, followed by a certain number of reps, with weight amount and speed of reps factoring into the process. In between each set there is a break, maybe a minute or two, and then the next set commences. This continues for the duration of the workout. Considering that muscle and strength gains come quickly for beginners, if their introduction to resistance training is high-volume, and if the results fall within their goals, they will continue this way of training because it yielded results and everyone else is training this way. If their initial introduction to training was HIT, would they eventually transition to high volume training?

HIT requires a mental shift away from sets and reps, and towards time under load. When you make this shift, you stop counting reps and decrease the number of sets. This significantly cuts down on the time spent exercising. Initially it may be difficult to move away from HVT because a much briefer path towards strength and muscle building may seem unrealistic for someone who has trained the HVT way for long time. I went through this mental process, made the shift, and eventually nailed down a very specific home training system guided by HIT principles which works very well for me.

If You Are New to Resistance Training and HIT

Please be mindful that the information in this book is from the perspective and experience of someone who had already performed resistance training for many years before discovering HIT and had personal trained others in both high volume and high-intensity modalities. If you are reading this and considering incorporating HIT as your exercise modality (which I hope you are), but have never performed any resistance training, I suggest a slow approach to this process, similar to what is utilized successfully in eccentric exercise therapeutic interventions. Considering the eccentric or negative phase of a movement is key to HIT (more on this soon), guidance from research within the eccentric exercise therapeutic realm makes sense. The work of Harris-Love et al. (2021) provides guidance for a phased approach, with the phases being comprised of familiarization, acclimatization, and progression. Becoming familiar with resistance exercise and specifically the slower repetitions associated with HIT would include two to three initial exercise sessions with low workloads, meaning less weight. This also provides the opportunity to develop proper form. Acclimating involves another week or two before finally progressing to a challenging enough weight resistance that would constitute an appropriate HIT stimulus.

If financially feasible, incorporating a personal trainer into this process can be beneficial, specifically to learn how to use weight machines in the gym. In a perfect world, you'll be able to locate a HIT-specific studio close to where you live and learn directly from a HIT personal trainer. Researching HIT training videos on-line may be helpful as well.

High-Intensity Principles

There are several important principles to understand regarding high-intensity training. They can be incorporated into workouts with machines and free weights, as well as body weight exercises:

1. Use a challenging weight – if you are a beginner to resistance training this may take a bit to assess and figure out. Ideally, you'll find a weight amount via which you will reach muscular failure within 45 to 90 seconds. The time under load (TUL) is the length of the set from the moment you begin to when you can no longer move the weight (McGuff & Little 2009). If you exceed two minutes per set, consider raising the amount of weight. Don't count reps, focus on the TUL instead.

2. Slow repetition cadence – the goal is to negate momentum. The authors of *Body by Science* recommend between a six to 10 second positive lifting phase and a six to 10 second negative phase, with the totality of that constituting one repetition. You can have a faster cadence, around three to four seconds, as well. Along with the slow cadence, you must have proper form for each exercise, which will enhance safety and the overall impact of the exercise.

3. Training to failure – although ideally each HIT set is taken to failure, you don't have to go to absolute failure to attain benefits from high-intensity training. Efforts should be made to reach muscular failure if it can be done safely.

For the past four and a half years, I've used these principles with free weights and body weight exercises at home, to great success. Instead of moving the weights quickly as in HVT, I slow down the repetitions to eliminate momentum and go to muscular failure or as close to it as possible. When you utilize HIT, per Dr. McGuff, a good way to assess whether you are passing the threshold and recruited all necessary muscle fibers, is to perform a three-second positive and six-second negative cadence set. As you progress through the set, once your speed start to slow down on the positive portion of the set and you go above three seconds, you've succeeded in inroading the muscle.

As mentioned, machines simplify the high-intensity training process. The machine provides more incremental weight options, enhanced control of the movement, and most importantly, enhances safety. When using free weights, a training partner can enhance the workout by being a support and spotter. Whether you use machines or free weights, proper form is essential to get the most out of each repetition and avoid injury. Another benefit to high-intensity training is enhancement of the cardiovascular system. As McGuff and Little point out, "your cardiorespiratory system services the mechanical functioning of your muscles. Thus, the higher the intensity of muscular work, the higher the degree of cardiovascular and respiratory stimulation (p. 87)." They argue that challenging the muscles to work harder through high-intensity training provides metabolic improvements that go beyond any benefits from steady-state, longer-duration, and low-intensity activity. If you are currently asking yourself whether the incorporation of high-intensity resistance is adequate to not only replace high-volume training but also "cardio" exercise, the answer is – yes. In a 1998 article, HIT expert Drew Baye quotes Arthur Jones as saying, "six weeks of proper weight training can improve one's cardiovascular fitness to a degree that is impossible with any number of years of aerobics." Once you begin performing HIT workouts, especially if you choose to move from exercise to exercise with very short breaks in between, you will experience the impact of the workout not only on your muscles, but also on your "cardio".

Eccentric or Negative Movement

One very important aspect of resistance training that is sometimes overlooked is the eccentric or negative portion of the repetition. The slow cadence required during HIT guarantees that the negative portion of the repetition will be fully realized. An example of this is when you lower the weight on a barbell curl, elongating the muscle in the process. As Arthur Jones stated, "There's no doubt in my mind that for the purpose of building muscular size and strength, negative work is far more important than positive work" (Darden 2004, p. 25). In *The New High-intensity Training*, Ellington Darden points out that negative resistance exercise involves more muscle fibers. It also provides more stretching to the muscles and connective tissues. A 2009 systematic review by Roig et al. comparing eccentric to concentric resistance training found that eccentric training was superior for strength and muscle mass. Hedayatpour and Falla (2015) found that eccentric exercise adaptations contribute to improved muscle function. Fully realizing the entire repetition versus over-focusing on the positive portion of the movement can greatly enhance the impact of the exercise.

The eccentric movement is also where a larger portion of the muscle fiber damage occurs. For eventual muscle growth and strength increase, the muscle is stressed to the point where it needs repair, a byproduct of mechanical tension. The negative movement provides that stimulus more so than the positive. Considering that eccentric exercise may lead to temporary strength loss, decrease in range of motion, and soreness (Stozer at el. 2020), providing adequate time for recovery, which we'll address later, is essential to properly benefit from HIT.

Incorporating negatives in training can be done in several ways. One method is the one already discussed – the slow cadence of movement. Another method is to perform the positive movement quickly, maybe one or two seconds, and the negative slowly. A third option is to simply perform negative only sets. Consider this example for a negative only dip (you'll need something to stand on that will assist in starting at the top of the movement): begin in the top position of the dip. Now lower yourself slowly, around five to 10 seconds, until your shoulders are below your elbows. Once you reach the bottom of the movement, you stop, step back up on whatever you were standing on, and return to the top position before lowering yourself slowly again.

Most who resistance train have likely used momentum to their advantage, or more appropriately, disadvantage. It seems like an advantage at first because added momentum assists in the performance of a repetition and the more reps the better, right? Well, if these reps are not performed correctly due to the overuse of momentum, one is not getting the most out of the exercise. Once the repetition is slowed down to the point where momentum is eliminated, the targeted muscles do all the work. Even though momentum is fantastic in many other aspects of life, it serves no purpose when it comes to resistance exercise.

Fit20

The first Fit20 studio opened in 2009 in the Netherlands and since has expanded to 160 studios around the world. The training program requires its members to resistance train for only 20 minutes per week with a personal trainer utilizing high-intensity training concepts. The weekly training sessions are tracked to assess progress. Does it work? Research conducted on 14,690 Fit20 participants, 40 years of age and older, displayed a 30 to 50 percent increase in strength over the first year of training (Steele at el. 2021). The researchers concluded that "substantial strength gains are possible with the use of a minimal dose resistance training approach" (p. 28).

As I read more about Fit20 and its similarities to the high-intensity principles I learned about and incorporated in my home gym, I felt the urge to experience this workout. Only problem was there were no studios within New Jersey's borders, nor any in the tri-state area. The closest studio was in Virginia. When I found this out, I had to ask myself a very important question: Would I drive across four states for a 20-minute workout? The answer: Absolutely! The nearest location was in Fairfax Station, a 340-mile round trip. I sent an email inquiry to the studio, received a quick response via email and text, and had my workout scheduled for 12pm in late March 2024. The rainy, traffic-laden drive was less than optimal but the experience well worth the journey.

I met my Fit20 personal trainer in front of the studio. He looked the part, which was good, as passing the eye test holds value for anyone who is in the fitness industry. The studio was a rather small space with two rooms: an entry room with the main desk followed by the main room which was a bright space consisting of six nautilus machines, a water cooler, and a standing desk. The six machines were as follows: chest press, pull-down, leg press, ab crunch, back extension, and hip abductor/adductor. It was a pleasure to see the Nautilus brand in all its updated glory.

My trainer discussed the workout that he was going to guide me through, which began with the chest press. The nautilus machine weight was in kilograms, so we adjusted it accordingly taking into consideration the weight that I've used for my home chest workouts – 70kg or 154lbs. It doesn't seem like much for an experienced trainee, but when you move this amount very slowly, it gets arduous rather quickly. And slowly I would go – the trainer explained that a Fit20 workout is always 10-second positive and 10 seconds negative for each rep, with a 10-second hold at the end (this is the higher end of the high-intensity principles for cadence). It is one set only per machine and ideally the set is to complete muscular failure before the two-minute mark, preferably around the 90-second sweet spot. As I set myself up for the chest press, I noticed a small screen attached to the machine, a couple feet away from me, at face level. What popped up next on the screen ensured that I maintained the 10-second positive, 10-second negative cadence. My trainer held an iPad device with which he adjusted my range of motion for the exercise to my physique and input data for this set to assess progress over time (if I were to be a regular member). Once everything was ready, I positioned myself, nodded my head that I was ready to go, and a countdown began on the screen in front of me. The second I started the exercise, two bars appeared on the screen, moving slowly from left to right, one on top signifying the progression of the 10 seconds in real time and a second below showing my rate of movement. The goal was to ensure that my bar moved at the same speed as the top bar. Prior experience with slow reps helped me adjust quickly. I ended up going to complete muscular failure in 1:37, right around the sweet spot. This was phenomenal for a first try and my chest was cooked.

The trainer guided me through the rest of the machines, and although I did not hit the sweet spot for muscular failure every time, which makes sense considering it was my first time there and I did not have an established baseline for each machine, the workout was still challenging and impactful. Afterwards, I spoke with the trainer about the population that this specific studio attracted. He stated that most of his clients are between 40 and 80 years of age (the location and marketing of this studio has something to do with this), with some utilizing the Fit20 workout as a form of rehabilitation. This displays how safe HIT is, and at the same time impactful for strength and muscle gains. In their brochure, Fit20 touts the same health benefits as the classic high-intensity training outlined by McGuff and Little – including strength and energy increase, improved metabolism, stronger bones, decreased stress, and enhanced endurance. Interestingly, weight loss was not directly mentioned. Weight loss and exercise will be discussed in later chapters.

The Perfect Workout

Imagine a day after driving across four States and back to exercise, you find a high-intensity training studio 5.3 miles from your house. This is exactly what happened when during an internet search for more HIT training programs, I stumbled upon The Perfect Workout. With over 60 studios in the United States, I lucked out with the only one in New Jersey existing in the town next over from mine. I checked out the website and scheduled an introductory free session for the next day. The Perfect Workout opened its doors in 1999 on the West Coast and has expanded significantly over the past twenty-five years. Like Fit20, the program consists of personal training-only studios which utilize HIT principles for all workouts. Unlike Fit20, The Perfect Workout recommends two 20-minute workouts per week.

I walked into a large office building and located the studio on the bottom floor. The first thing I noticed upon entering the studio was the sign above the front desk – "What Doesn't Challenge You, Doesn't Change You." As I looked around, I realized the Nautilus brand was used here as well. The trainer on site, Brooke, was guiding the client before me, a middle-aged woman, through the pull-down machine while tracking her progress. After their workout concluded, I spoke with Brooke for a bit about The Perfect Workout philosophy and background. In the early 90s, after years of extensive time in the gym which led to varying benefits and unnecessary injuries, the founder discovered HIT and began incorporating it into his workouts, to great results. I asked about the cadence for each rep, and like Fit20, it was usually 10 seconds on the positive, 10 seconds on the negative, although Brooke advised that she was perfectly ok with a rep going even slower. The time sweet spot for each set was between 60 and 90 seconds, not to exceed two minutes, with one set only per exercise. Although there were no timers on the machines, Brooke kept track of the time and guided clients through each repetition. Every workout was closely tracked so the clients were aware of their progress. I asked about the age demographic that this studio attracted and was advised that it was 40 and over (like Fit20), which is partially due to the socioeconomic reality of being able to afford consistent personal training.

Considering I experienced a high-intensity training session two days earlier, with my intro session at this studio I leaned into one of the machines I didn't see at Fit20 – the preacher curl. Brooke loaded up the weight to 100lbs and I began to slowly raise the bar up to the top of the curl position, and slowly lowered it back down as she coached me through the first repetition. Since the cadence was around 10 seconds up and 10 seconds down, there weren't many more reps to be had and I hit failure at three reps, which lasted around 55 seconds. My biceps were cooked! Due to the variety of machines at this studio, the two 20-minute weekly sessions could be varied. At the end of the day, it all depended on the client, their abilities, needs, and progress. The Perfect Workout also provided a virtual training option via their website, which demonstrated that HIT is transferable to the home, as in my experience, and can still be impactful without the use of machines.

After the workout, I asked Brooke if the studio advertised weight loss as a benefit of the training. She advised it did not, and that there is a separate nutrition program available for that purpose. I thanked Brooke for her time and walked out the door feeling accomplished and happy to know that a quality expert-guided HIT workout was only 5.3 miles away.

Going to Failure

In his recent book, *Be Useful: Seven Tools for Life*, Arnold Schwarzenegger discussed the importance of reframing failure into a learning experience instead of a debilitating one. Any time we try something and fail the experience can serve as a measurement for how far we've come in our efforts, how much farther we need to go, and what we should do differently the next time around. Schwarzenegger points out that failure is built into weight training and that "the whole goal in weight lifting is to work your muscles to failure (p. 172)." When you can't complete another rep because your muscles are fully fatigued, it means that you had a good workout. In HIT, failure, or very close to it, is not only built into the process, but also a necessity. Any time you push your physical limits and fail during a HIT workout, you've succeeded. Schwarzenegger further states: "when failure is a positive part of the game you play, it's much less scary to search for the limits of your ability... (p. 173)". Resistance training, and specifically HIT workouts, may serve as a laboratory for becoming comfortable with failure so that we push ourselves to levels which we may not have felt comfortable going beyond in other aspects of life. We may notice that just like failure is part of the process for muscle growth and development, it is also a necessary step in our attempts at personal growth, worthy pursuits, and the achievement of success.

The Importance of Exercise Recovery

The result of using HIT principles properly is enhanced muscle strength and size, which will lead to increased functionality, healthy aging, and minimization of injury, along with a slew of other benefits. The process involves stressing the body to produce a positive adaptation, with the body's response to this stimulus being the key. Your body does not know what is going on when it's being taken to muscular failure other than that it is not equipped to handle such a stressor, hence after the experience, it needs to get stronger in case said stimulus occurs again. When you look at exercise from this perspective, it's clear that if the stimulus is impactful enough, it should not be utilized often. There are two parts to high-intensity training, and to any resistance training for that matter: the work and the recovery. Too often, there is an overemphasis on the work aspect of exercise because we tend to believe that the more we exercise, the better. This is a faulty perspective and can lead us down the road of over-training, lack of progress and muscle growth, and eventually injury. There is no infinite level of fitness that we should strive for. A point exists where striving for fitness can begin to negatively impact our health. This is where understanding the significance of adequate recovery time comes in.

The work portion of resistance training, that being movement against a specific weight, causes temporary damage to muscle fibers. Those fibers need time to rebuild to their pre-workout size, but ideally to a greater size. The recovery time can vary greatly, from five days to several weeks, but generally at least one full week is considered a good rest time for a muscle group that has been properly stressed (McGuff & Little 2009). Regular, quality sleep will enhance the recovery process. As one continues with HIT, it's important to assess progress. Are you able to perform your set beyond two minutes after a certain number of weeks? That is a sign it's time to up the weight. As you become stronger, the stimulus needs to increase accordingly. Tracking progress via a journal, app, or another format ensures that you attain maximum benefits from the time you are dedicating to exercise.

Getting Started with HIT

The simplest way to begin your HIT journey is with machines in a gym. Let's take the chest press for example. Begin by sitting down and aligning the seat accordingly to your height, so that you are pressing at chest level. Next, pick a weight that is challenging and grip the handles. Assume proper posture and begin pressing slowly, ideally somewhere between five to 10 seconds for the positive and the negative movements. Do not lock out your elbows nor stop at the top of the press. Instead, when you get close to locking out, begin to slowly bring the weight back towards your chest. Right before the weight rack touches, press out slowly again. Eventually the weight will become more difficult to move at the same cadence as your strength diminishes, which is a place where some people may want to stop. You will not stop here though. You'll continue to press until you are no longer able to, at which point you'll hold the weight in whatever position you've become stuck in, for an additional 10 seconds. After the 10 seconds, you'll lower the weight slowly and safely to the starting position. Congratulations, you've completed a set of HIT! This will likely not be the most enjoyable experience of your life, yet whatever it feels like is what you will need to be at peace with to successfully implement HIT long-term. The tradeoff for minimizing time is maximizing intensity.

The above is just one example, there are a myriad of exercises, whether you use machines, free weights, or body weight, that can serve as the starting point for HIT. Ensure that you utilize enough exercises to target all major muscle groups in a scheduled manner. As you experiment with the exercises remember that you are an explorer through this process, discovering what is going to work best for you.

Chapter 3

Transition of HIT & HIIT to the Home

COVID-Imposed Home Gym

In February 2020, the world was turned upside down. I vividly remember the rumors and discussions at work of a possible complete shutdown. Within a week of these conversations, I was home as the sole daytime caretaker for my four and six-year-old girls. A week later, the rest of my co-workers were sent home, and my wife was let go from her job. For the next two years, I spent over 95% of my time at home with my immediate family. Thankfully, the transition to this novel lifestyle was relatively smooth for us. We were blessed with each other and lucky to avoid any catastrophic illness to us and close family members.

When it came to health and self-care, major adjustments were needed. The local gym I was a member of shut down, as did the rest of the gyms. The State of New Jersey maintained extremely strict COVID guidelines for a significant amount of time. Gym owners adjusted via virtual personal/group training and outdoor training, but those options did not interest me. I had enough exercise equipment at home for a complete workout but as with most adjustments, could I muster the motivation to transition from the gym to home workouts only? I was a gym member for the past 20-plus years. Here were the motivational factors that propelled a successful transition and the reflection involved:

- I had worked in the field of nutrition and exercise for a long time and needed to continue passing the eye test of someone who works in this field.

- I wanted to continue looking good as I aged, so when I looked in the mirror, I could take pride in the outcome of all the hard work and effort that went into my training.

- I wanted to continue feeling good daily, to maintain functionality, and to avoid disease. I was in my 40s and wanted to continue feeling like someone in their 20s.

- I wanted to maintain the high level of confidence that the results of exercise had provided me, especially since my day job required speaking in front of groups of people on a regular basis.

- The long-distance view – in old age, I didn't want to be a burden to myself, my immediate family, and society. Exercise is a self-care strategy which can enhance health span.

- I wanted to continue my healthy lifestyle and to hopefully inspire others to incorporate exercise into their lives.

The cognitive behavioral model tells us that thoughts affect behavior. These thoughts were the drivers to continue exercising irrelevant of access to a gym. As you'll read in the chapter on motivation, they tap into all aspects of Self. Some of them are the exact thoughts that sparked my exercise journey when I was 19 years old. The benefits I attained from exercise over the years further reinforced my motivation to continue training at all costs. Having space and equipment for a home gym, as well as plenty of free time, made the process much easier.

Personal trainer and co-host of the podcast "Mind Pump", Sal DiStefano, is a big proponent of the home gym. Some of the home gym benefits he points out in his book, *The Resistance Training Revolution,* are convenience, comfort, personal choice of clothes, music, and the dissolvement of any self-consciousness of a gym environment with lots of fit and buff people walking around. From my experience this is all very accurate. When exercising at home, I fit my workouts in smoothly within my schedule at the ideal time and it only takes a few steps to get to the room where the home gym in located. I wear what I want, play whatever music I want as loud as I want, and can talk to myself without any questionable stares coming my way. My home gym is my sacred space and doubles as my work-from-home office. Even if you don't have a specific room in the home to dedicate to workout equipment, a part of your living space can easily serve that purpose. A yoga mat, bench, and some weights take up a surprisingly small amount of space.

Recent fitness polling data displays that home exercise may be here to stay, as more Americans are exercising at home versus the gym, with convenience as the strongest factor (Goodwin 2023). One important benefit of combining quick workouts with a home gym is an increase in the likelihood of exercising. "I don't have time" is no longer an excuse when you only need to carve out a few minutes a day, in your own home. The short workouts combined with convenience may increase motivation. If you schedule the ten minutes in the morning, let's say at 7:30am before you head out to work, and for some reason your morning routine doesn't go as planned, those ten minutes can easily fit into the post-work evening routine.

The equipment and motivation were there to exercise at home during COVID, but I was still home with my family 24-7. They needed my time and energy, and the best of me daily. The ten-minute home workouts I developed utilizing HIT principles were ideal for not only minimizing my exercise time, but also maximizing my time being a husband, father, and support system for my loved ones. And because of the workout benefits, I could spend that time with them feeling at or close to 100 percent every single day.

Home Gym Goods

Over the years, I've collected the following exercise equipment: the Tower of Power (pull-up bar, dip bar, and leg raise trifecta), the Power Block (compact) totaling two dumbbells with a max weight of 70 pounds each, an adjustable bench, stationary spin bike, a couple low weight kettle bells, resistance bands, the Ab Wheel, a stepper, stability ball, and medicine balls. This stuff takes up a surprisingly small amount of space. If I were to recommend essentials from these items, they would be the adjustable bench, the dumbbells, resistance bands, and a stability ball – a $400-$500 investment. Outside of utilizing this equipment, body weight exercises are an important part of the home workout routine.

Development of the Home HIT Routine

Considering I did not have a 3000 square foot gym space in my house to fit several Nautilus machines, I went into my exercise toolbox to create resistance workouts grounded in HIT philosophy while using free weights and body weight exercises with the equipment and within the space that I had. The following HIT principles were non-negotiable: slow, controlled reps to negate momentum, with cadence ranging anywhere from four to 10 seconds, challenging (yet not necessarily heavy) weight for the exercises, and going to or as close to complete muscular failure as possible without compromising safety. Some exercises, such as the dumbbell chest press, can become dangerous without a spotter when moving weight to failure, hence I used slow push-ups immediately after in an attempt to tap the deeper muscle fibers.

With respect to a training schedule, I broke my daily workouts into one muscle group per day, same as in my 20s and 30s in the gym, for ten minutes per workout. The 10 minutes included the time under load and rest periods. This equates to six workouts per week at 10 minutes each, totaling an hour dedicated to exercise each week. Once we subtract the rest periods from this number, the total time under load becomes approximately 20-30 minutes a week, or three to five minutes a day. I targeted the following muscle groups directly once a week: legs, chest, shoulders, biceps/triceps, and back. Sometimes the workouts lasted less than the allocated timeframe of 10 minutes, especially when I slowed the cadence down to 10 seconds positive/10 seconds negative. My body responded well to targeting each muscle group once per week, but you may want to experiment how often you target them.

Why 10 minutes per workout, six days a week? Because that's what worked and still works best for me for the following reasons:

- **Convenience** – I could easily relegate 10 minutes a day to exercise. With such a short time, there were zero time-related reasons not to work out.

- **Schedule** – I liked to exercise in the morning, especially when I commuted to work. I usually worked out between 6:50am and 7:00am. Research on the best times to exercise is contradictory. Throughout my life, I've exercised starting as early as 6am to as late as 9pm, and everywhere in between. At this point in my life, exercise aligns best with my mornings.

- **Mindset** – HIT is not fun nor is it pleasant. Considering this, it was easier to be mentally prepped to target one muscle group per day, versus a whole-body workout once per week or two split routines. Working out at home made this feasible.

- **Results** – I liked how I looked and felt! To this day, I am fascinated by the amazing results of such a short exercise stimulus. The home workouts were (and still are) so effective for me, once gyms reopened after the height of COVID, I continued to exercise at home only.

Following is MY home workout routine. Please consider this important point from HIT expert Drew Baye: HIT is not a program; it is a set of principles. The below is an example of the application of HIT principles. Based on your goals, schedule, age, body type, genetics, recovery time, expertise, and other factors, you may benefit more from other exercises, using machines in the gym, targeting a muscle group less or more often than once a week, doing a full body workout in one day or split routine over two days, etc. Consider that each set I perform doesn't go past two minutes and that I vary the cadence. I have tested one, two, and even three sets per body part, have incorporated other exercises (such as dips and the ab wheel Bob Backlund style for triceps), and occasionally high-volume for specific exercises.

(Note: for the past few months, I've used a 10 second positive, 10 second negative cadence only, 2 total sets per workout for each of the exercises below, except back):

Day One – Legs – wall squat with stability ball for back support while holding dumbbells, cadence five to 10 seconds positive, five to 10 second negative.

Day Two – Chest – dumbbell presses, cadence five to 10 seconds positive, five to 10 second negative, (take safety of exercise under consideration), followed immediately by slow cadence push-ups, 10 seconds positive, 10 second negative till failure.

Day Three – Biceps – seated dumbbell curls, cadence five to 10 -second positive, five to 10-second negative, followed immediately by static 90-degree chin-up hold on pull-up bar until body naturally lowers.

Day Four – Shoulders – dumbbell shoulder presses, cadence five to 10-second positive, five to 10-second negative, followed immediately by side extensions using resistance band, cadence five to 10-seconds till failure.

Day Five – Triceps – laying dumbbell extensions on bench, cadence five to 10-second positive, five to 10-second negative, (taking safety of exercise under consideration), followed immediately by triceps extension with 40-50lb resistance band suspended from pull-up bar, five to 10-second positive and negative till failure.

Day Six – Back (advanced workout) – one-minute chin-up or pull-up, 30 seconds up, 30 seconds down, usually two sets and a static chin-up or pull-up hold to finish, OR high-volume: 100 chin-ups or pull-ups, 10 sets of 10 reps in under 10 minutes.

If You Use HIT In the Gym

I don't expect anyone to drive to the gym, however long it takes, for eight to 10-minute workouts, six days a week, and drive back home. The above home routine is convenient for me and keeps me motivated to train. If you are going to incorporate HIT in the gym, whether it's using machines or free weights, you can combine all these exercises into one or two days. Use machines that target the major muscle groups, such as the leg press, chest press, or pull-down. If you are using free weights or body weight, that would equate to the bench press, squat, and chin up. How often should you work out? That depends on your recovery time and if you are indeed tapping the deeper muscle fibers during the workouts. Leaning towards the "less, is more" principle will likely lead to better results. As you get stronger, you'll need to raise the weight to continue stimulating progress. Even though I target one muscle group per week, for you it may be different depending on the rate of recovery, and other individual factors already mentioned.

Eliminate the Ego

As mentioned earlier, one important aspect of resistance training that is often overlooked is the negative portion of the movement. Gym goers, specifically men, tend to assess their training progression on the number of reps they pump out and/or the amount of weight they can mobilize, which may lead to the overfocus on these aspects of resistance training. Often, the ego will connect with the number of reps and/or heaviness of weight for the gauging of progression. Ego-driven resistance training can lead to compromised form and injury. I have friends in their 40s who still talk about how much weight they can lift. This was maybe cool in our 20s when we didn't know any better, but as we get older, it's a fantastic recipe for getting hurt. Moving away from ego-driven training towards training that is focused on results without the showtime, is a step in the right direction. Once we eliminate ego from the formula, we can fully focus on the movement, proper form, safety, and results of each exercise. HIT is not about moving weight; it is about utilizing the weight to properly stimulate the muscles. In this mind space, we can begin to better appreciate the negative portion of a resistance movement. Furthermore, when moving any weight while performing resistance training, it's essential to stay mentally connected to the physical action to reduce the chance of injury. Over time and with more practice, keen focus while performing HIT will become second nature.

Stay Open-Minded and Don't Throw Away Tools

The exercises I perform are not set in stone as the toolbox is always open for the implementation of new things, or the return of old. Currently, HIT is perfect for what I need when it comes to exercise and although I cannot predict the future, it's hard to see myself moving away from it. However, I always stay open to new things and am willing to give most a fair shot. Maybe a new exercise will become my favorite or maybe it'll end up buried at the bottom of the toolbox, only to be rediscovered years later. There are certain things that I've tried to implement such as Turkish get-ups, static stretching, and yoga. They didn't stick; maybe the time wasn't right, but that doesn't mean that they are completely ineffective. Other exercises such as planks have benefited me greatly in the past, but I haven't used them regularly for a few years now. I still use volume training for pull-ups and chin-ups. Staying open-minded enhances the opportunity to learn new things, whether we find them worthy of long-term implementation or not.

 A little bit about exercise and the world wide web: the excessive amount of entertaining "exercise" routines on the internet is truly fascinating. Sadly, a lot of time the individuals performing these exercises are doing it for clicks and likes, not to demonstrate something effective that most people can do. I'm happy that some of these folks can perform a perfect squat while standing on a stability ball, with a 45lb plate around their waist, while they shoulder press a barbell. That certainly sounds like doable fun, for exactly no one! On the other hand, watching someone perform a HIT routine is not prime entertainment, maybe even slightly unexciting, but it's sure darn effectively efficient. Hence, try not to get overly mesmerized by the workout bells and whistles on the internet, especially if it's something that only .00001% of the population can perform. Thankfully, most people can safely perform HIT.

Planks

A major factor associated with the discontinuation of exercise as we age is pain and injuries. Examples include chronic back pain, or any other discomfort associated with the spinal cord, wear-and-tear from years of dynamic and excessive exercise, an acute injury that has impacted range of motion, strength, and/or mobility of a certain body part, or tightness and lack of mobility due to a sedentary lifestyle. Being in pain sucks and can be the determining factor as to whether someone plants themselves on the couch after work or is willing and able to move. I can relate to this as scoliosis combined with poor posture early in my life lead to significant back pain in my 20s. I could not wash dishes for more than five minutes at a time without feeling sharp pain in my lower back, and always wore a heavy-duty weight belt for back stability when performing shoulder presses and bicep curls in the gym. I distinctly remember being in excruciating pain at several standing-room-only music concerts. Eventually I discovered planking and resolved my back pain through years of performing this exercise by progressively extending the timeframe that I would plank for. I started with 30 seconds per plank and eventually reached a personal best of seven minutes. Planking strengthened my core muscles, and I was able to ditch the back support weight belt at the gym for good. I'm also able to stand for long periods of time without experiencing intense pain. Research findings support the use of planks for reduction of lower back pain (Kline 2013). Amazingly, I have not planked for several years but have maintained the benefits of the exercise. Since planks take only minutes to perform, it makes sense to put them into the effectively efficient exercise toolbox.

High-Intensity Interval Training (HIIT)

There is one more piece to the effectively efficient workout puzzle, and that is high-intensity interval training (HIIT). HIIT has been around in some capacity for one hundred years, initially championed by competitive athletes. The formal definition of HIIT provides a clear description: "a form of exercise in which short periods of extremely demanding physical activity are alternated with less intense recovery periods." This is the training system that Roger Bannister used to become the first person to break the four-minute mile (Gibala 2017). The great thing about HIIT is that aside from its benefits for professional athletes, it can be utilized by most for fitness and health enhancement. For a full understanding and appreciation of HIITs impact, it's important to discuss McMaster University in Canada and the work of Dr. Martin Gibala.

In the early 2000s, Gibala conducted ground-breaking experiments which displayed how powerful interval training is compared to steady-state endurance aerobic exercise. One of the experiments displayed that around ten minutes of HIIT a week provided the same fitness improvements as four and a half hours of continuous moderate intensity exercise per week. The measurements for this experiment included aerobic fitness, increased mitochondria in the muscles, and ability to burn fat during exercise. Another experiment showed that "...a total of just 18 minutes of very intense exercise produced the same benefits as 10.5 hours of traditional endurance training (Gibala 2017, p. 40)." These mind-blowing findings displayed the importance of exercise intensity versus duration. The paradigm that more is better was flipped on its head.

High-intensity interval training involves an all-out physical exertion over a short span of time, followed by a much lesser exertion. The amount of these intervals between high and low intensity can vary depending on the workout. What exactly is an all-out physical exertion? The exertion rating chart in Gibala' book, *The One-Minute Workout*, is an excellent tool for figuring this out. The chart ranges from zero to 10+. An exertion level of three, considered moderate, would be defined by deeper breathing with the ability to form full sentences while exercising.

At level five, one starts to breath heavy and becomes uncomfortable. At level seven, one experiences rapid breathing and a preference not to talk and at level nine, one starts to gasp for air and is unable to speak. Level 10 and above, one exerts as hard as they possibly can, as in escaping danger. Consider level 10 as the epitome of the fight or flight response and you're a hunter-gatherer who's chosen flight from the saber-tooth wolverine creature that has targeted you for their sustenance.

Gibala provides specific workouts as well, ranging from beginner at lower exertion levels to more advanced at higher levels of exertion. Prior to implementing any exercise regimen, especially one where you are pushing yourself hard, please check with your doctor before you begin the program. Also conduct a self-assessment of your current fitness level so that you don't hurt yourself or begin with unrealistic expectations. I recommend a stationary bicycle as the safest equipment to perform HIIT, as it minimizes impact and lessens overall chance of injury. Another option is sprints, which are more high impact.

The following "advanced routine" was used by Gibala and his team in an experiment, three times a week and tested against 150 minutes a week of traditional endurance training:

> Two-minute warm-up, 20-second sprint, two-minute light, 20-second sprint, two-minute light, 20-second sprint, and three-minute cool down. Total time: 10 minutes with a total of one-minute all-out 10+ exertion (p. 172)

The results? You guessed it, the same for both. One minute of all-out exertion three times a week improved cardiorespiratory fitness, increased muscle mitochondria, and decreased body fat percentage, and improved blood sugar management the same as 150 minutes of steady-state aerobic exercise.

Ten minutes total is cool, but can we lower the total time of the workout while still maintaining the high-intensity bursts which are the all-important aspect of HIIT? Of course. The great part about any workout, exercise, etc. is that outside the recommended routines, which are provided as a template, as long as we maintain the integrity of the exercise philosophy, it can be adjusted for our purposes. Below is my version of a HIIT workout on a stationary spin bike:

Thirty-second warm-up, 30-second sprint, two-minute slow pedaling, 30-second sprint, two-minute slow pedaling, 30-second sprint. Total time: six minutes, one and a half minutes all out 10+ exertion.

In my routine above, I've increased the one-minute workout with total exertion time and minimized the rest time. I felt comfortable making the adjustment based on my fitness level. You may adjust the routine for your specific fitness level, needs, and goals. In the future, I may include a cool down, more high-intensity bursts, etc. It's always great to continue challenging the body if you notice adaptation to exercise stimuli. Eventually it may be time for me to add a fourth 10+ exertion level sprint. Adding one 30-second burst is certainly effectively efficient!

When using a stationary bike for HIIT, the level of resistance will greatly impact how challenging the workout will be. I prefer a medium level of resistance. My heart rate is usually at 90% of max or slightly above once I finish my six-minute HIIT routine. Breathing is labored and takes a few minutes to recover. I feel muscle activation in my lower body, predominantly the glutes, hamstrings, and quads. This is not a pleasant experience but again, it's only three thirty-second sets of discomfort. Am I willing to put myself through this to significantly shorten my workouts? Absolutely! Are you willing to do the same or would you prefer to sit on a bike for 30-40 minutes and steady state pedal for the same fitness benefits? That's a hard pass for me, plus those stationary bike seats can do a number on the buttocks.

The Complete Tool Box

We began this exercise journey with Bob Backlund's Harvard Step Test and Ab Wheel variation. Next, we reviewed the difference between HVT and HIT, followed by a deeper look at HIT. Lastly, we discussed high-intensity interval training. The path to efficiency and attainment of exercise benefits in the shortest time possible points directly to HIT and HIIT. This does not mean that other types of exercise are unworthy of assessment and utilization. If it's safe, go for it! As mentioned before, I still use the Ab Wheel as taught to me by Bob because I find its phenomenal for working the triceps. I still use high-volume training for certain muscle groups due to the limitation of equipment in my home gym. It doesn't make sense to completely discard these philosophies and exercises as they hold value in the present and likely will in the future.

Chapter 4

Health Benefits of Exercise

HIT Health Benefits

If proper stimuli and recovery are utilized using HIT, muscle growth will be the result. Regarding the benefits of muscle, McGuff and Little state the following in *Body by Science*:

> The 'health' territory that muscle tissue covers is phenomenal. It includes the potential for processing waste materials, oxygenating blood, controlling insulin levels, optimizing bone-mineral density, increasing metabolic rate, reducing bodyfat levels, optimizing aerobic capacity, enhancing flexibility, and appreciably reducing the chances of injury, while at the same time allowing you to perform day-to-day tasks with far less wear and tear and stress on your body. All these health benefits flow from the building and strengthening of your muscles. (p. 97)

Further support for the benefits of strong muscles comes from Dr. Al Sears' *P.A.C.E.: The 12-minute Fitness Revolution*. Sears specifically mentions alleviation of back pain and improvement in personal appearance, self-esteem, and self-confidence. Sears recommends brief exercises within the realm of HIIT for aerobic fitness and body-weight resistance exercises for muscle building, fat loss, and functionality.

Considering the above benefits are tied directly to the growth and maintenance of muscle, any effective resistance training program can yield these physiological benefits. If you have the time and motivation to spend one hour a day in the gym for HVT, ensuring that you are not over-training and are recovering properly, you will build muscle and enjoy the health benefits associated with resistance training. Yet you can absolutely do the same in a much shorter time through the implementation of HIT.

The growth and maintenance of muscle as you age equals a healthier, fitter, better you. The day-to-day noticeable benefits are more strength, firmer muscles, clothes fitting better, more energy, and possibly a few inches off the waist. Aside from these physical benefits there are also psychological ones, including the already mentioned increases in confidence and self-esteem, as well as pride, grit, and enhanced mood. Weight loss is likely to occur as well due to the increase in metabolic rate, although focusing solely on weight loss can become problematic if the scale is not moving. Connecting our motivation to the non-weight loss noticeable physical benefits will likely enhance the chance that we stick with HIT long-term. The psychological benefits serve as further drivers to continue training.

HIIT Health Benefits

In *The One Minute Workout*, Gibala states the following: "The physiological changes that come with exercise and enable us to run faster and harder in the short term, also help us live longer and more active lives – with less chronic disease (p. 71)." Mankind has made great strides in the past one hundred years or so in the fields of engineering and medicine. This progress has greatly enhanced life expectancy, although being on this planet longer may not equate to an overall pleasant experience, especially in the last 10-15 years of life. Too often, chronic disease greatly impacts the quality of life for individuals who live to and beyond the average life expectancy, specifically in the United States. Hence, even though life span has been enhanced, our health span has not followed suit. Health span is the years in a person's life when they are in generally good health. Every person's long-term health and wellness goal should be to ensure that their life span and health span are the same length of time. Sometimes, circumstances beyond our control make this goal difficult to accomplish, but if we have control over our health, it is a worthy pursuit. Otherwise, if life span and health span are not in alignment, whatever number of years the individual spends ill, in pain, and/or unable to fully enjoy their existence, takes a heavy toll on that person, their immediate family, and society.

Regular exercise is one method that can mitigate the onset of chronic disease and subsequent decline in middle and later years. In his book, Dr. Gibala cites several research studies that demonstrate HIIT's profound effects on two specific chronic diseases: cardiovascular disease and type 2-diabetes. With respect to the cardiovascular system, exercise can slow down the natural degeneration of this system as we age, with HIIT being especially impactful for this purpose. With type-2 diabetes, one of Gibala's studies demonstrated that "interval training is a potent way to help people manage their blood sugar and decrease the symptoms of insulin resistance and type 2-diabetes (p. 92)." Steady state cardio exercise can provide these benefits as well, although in some head-to-head comparisons, HIIT was deemed more potent. Further benefits of HIIT include activating autophagy, the body's internal cleaning system that gets rid of damaged cells and old proteins (Hyman 2023).

Exercise as We Age

In his recent New York Times best seller, *Outlive: The Science & Art of Longevity*, Dr. Peter Attia discussed the importance of exercise for extending our health span. Through exercise we can reverse both physical and cognitive decline. Attia also pointed out that study after study shows that individuals who exercise regularly can live up to a decade longer than sedentary people. He sees value in both resistance and aerobic training and ties the benefits of both to functionality in old age. Considering all of us will experience eventual age-related physical decline, it makes sense to set a high health baseline earlier in life, specifically when it comes to muscle mass and strength. Although it's admirable to begin a training program later in life, the older we get, the more difficult it is to build muscle. Another important benefit of resistance training, specifically with heavy weights, is stimulation of bone growth. This holds great value as we age, considering how problematic a fracture can be later in life.

Specific to HIT, and even when starting in older age, eccentric exercise, or the negative portion of the movement, has been shown to provide significant health benefits. In their research overview of eccentric exercise, Love-Harris et al. (2021) stated that eccentric force declines at a slower rate than concentric force with aging, and that eccentric exercise has found a place as "an appealing treatment option for maintaining and/or improving neuromuscular health and physical function in older adults" (p. 6). They further state that eccentric exercise provides improvement in skeletal muscle structure, strength, power, balance, stair decent, and fall risk in older adults.

Is consistent exercise applied over many decades the only path towards golden years of functionality? It can be, but ideally, exercise is combined with other strategies. Take, for instance, my 88-year-old barber, Joey. Joey wakes up at 5am in the morning and begins the day with 100 leg crunches before he gets out of bed. He eats a light breakfast consisting of a few pieces of fruit and heads over to his barbershop to cut hair from 6am to 6pm. Regular exercise has been a part of Joey's life for over 60 years, but there are other factors that keep him going and motivated to continue working twelve hours, on his feet, four days a week. Joey is driven by purpose, and in the simplest terms, by the need to help others. He is also a firm believer in the importance of setting goals as well as waking up every day striving to be better than the previous day. His interactions with people are always pleasant as he spends his free time during work hours in front of his shop saying hi and mingling with everyone who walks by. That's how I became his client twelve years ago. Joey also focuses a lot of his time on family, which consists of his wife, daughters, and grandchildren. Joey's way of life shows that focusing efforts on exercise and movement is important but just one piece of the puzzle. Having a reason and purpose to get up every single morning, and surrounding ourselves with quality people, both family and friends, is going to greatly enhance our chances of enjoying our golden years and extending health span.

It's likely that most of us would like to spend as much time on this planet as we can, for a myriad of reasons. We are all aware of the eventual finality of life, although for some the true reflection of mortality occurs too close to the actual outcome. I believe there are benefits to being fully in touch with our mortality early enough to develop a full appreciation for the short amount of time that we are here. Of course, there are other paths to develop this appreciation. My personal reflection on the brevity of life has spurred the goal for maintenance of both mental and physical functionality for as long as possible. I want to possess the capacity for learning, movement, and production into old age to extend the amount of time that I can positively impact others. I also do not want to burden my family with having to take care of me. This is a huge motivator for the continued implementation of all matters of self-care in my life. When I visualize myself, in my 80s, I see a nimble old man, tending to the garden and landscaping around his home. He's fully functional, moving around spryly and smoothly. He possesses some semblance of muscle tone and good posture. He feels great. Will this eventually become reality? Hopefully, but it's good to know that I have significant control over the materialization of this mental image.

Brain Benefits of Exercise

Considering exercise is a physical activity, appreciation for its benefits is often relegated to physical changes obvious to the naked eye, as discussed already. Yet, there are many game-changing benefits which we cannot see because they are internal, specifically in the brain. In his book, *Spark: The Revolutionary New Science of Exercise and the Brain*, Dr. John Ratey shares significant insight into the fascinating positive impact of exercise on the brain.

One of the day-to-day activities that exercise's enhancement of brain neurochemistry positively impacts is learning. As Ratey explains in his book, exercise,

> ...optimizes your mindset to improve alertness, attention, and motivation; second, it prepares and encourages nerve cells to bind to one another, which is the cellular basis for logging in new information; and third, it spurs the development of new nerve cells from stem cells in the hippocampus. (p. 53)

The bottom line is this: exercise enhances our ability to learn. Further brain benefits of exercise discussed by Ratey include enhancement of the body's ability to deal with stress, alleviate the symptoms of anxiety disorders, counteract depression, enhance focus for people with ADHD, combat addiction, and slow down cognitive decline. All these benefits can be life-altering for anyone who is either dealing with mental health issues or wants to use exercise as a preventative measure.

Ratey points out further physiological benefits of exercise such as regulation of insulin in the body and immune system enhancement. By incorporating physical activity in our lives, we also become more social beings.

Ratey's exercise recommendations for attainment of the benefits described above span the full scope of physical exertion, from walking to HIIT, with a focus on aerobic activity. One of the benefits of HIIT he points out is the pituitary gland's release of human growth hormone (HGH) during high-intensity training. As Ratey explains,

The levels of HGH naturally secreted into the bloodstream decreases over your life span, so that by middle age they dwindle to a tenth of what they were during childhood, for both men and women. And a sedentary lifestyle exasperates this decline: high levels of cortisol, insulin resistance, and excess fatty acids in the bloodstream all clamp down further on the hormone's release. HGH is the body's master craftsman, burning belly fat, layering on muscle fiber, and pumping up brain volume. (p. 256)

Considering the immense positive impact of HGH, we would be remiss not to naturally tap into this protein. Ratey also cited a study which used the same exact HIIT stimulus that I incorporate on the spin bike: thirty-second all out sprints. The results: a sixfold increase in HGH, which peaks two hours after the exercise.

The incorporation of regular resistance training into one's life also provides benefits for the brain. Neurogenesis, the creation of new neurons, and neuroplasticity, the ability to form new connections and pathways, are two benefits of resistance training specific to the brain. Brain derived neurotrophic factor (BDNF) has been shown to have positive effects on neurogenesis and neuroplasticity (Current 2021). A 2017 study found that to-fatigue based resistance training provides the stimulus to increase peripheral serum BDNF (Marston at el.). Along with these physical health benefits are mental health ones, which include improved concentration, enhanced cognitive function, boosted creativity, boosted long-term memory, enhanced mood, protection against dementia and depression, and alleviation of stress and anxiety (Current 2021).

When assessing any exercise philosophy or system, one must always consider safety as integral to the final decision on whether to incorporate the exercise. For example, if long distance running hurts your knees, this is not the best exercise for you because it exasperates a knee issue irrelevant of any cardiovascular health benefits associated with running. The effort to enhance health is neutralized by the negative impact of the activity on the body. If an exercise hurts in a way that it's not supposed to, stop doing it. Considering most people who run have poor form, one can research the proper way to run and see if that will negate the knee pain or simply transition to the bike for either steady state exercise if you want to spend the time, or sprints. My suggestion: save yourself the time and do the HIIT sprints! If you want to greatly minimize the chance of injury while exercising, HIT is a great option.

A Real World Workout with Bob

As we were wrapping up our interview with a summary of the positive impact of exercise, Bob stated that it was time for us to go have a real-world workout. I had exactly zero clue what was in store but proceeded to go out into the "real world" and see what exactly Bob had in store for me. As I stood outside taking in the pleasant weather, I noticed Bob approaching with an ax in his hand. He told me that he has a chainsaw but prefers chopping wood with an ax, which he considers a nice change of pace from his regular workouts. We walked into a nearby wooded area by his house until Bob located a fallen tree. He positioned himself above it and proceeded to chop cleanly through it in exactly one minute and seven seconds – again, at the age of 69. Twenty seconds later, Bob tossed the ax in my general direction, accompanied by a hearty "you're next!" I was again caught off guard but had only one choice with the camera rolling – time to chop, baby! Bob's performance set the bar rather high and considering I was a wood chopping novice, it was difficult to prognosticate my level of wood chopping success.

 I started chopping and continued to chop beyond Bob's benchmark time performance. I have no idea how long I chopped for, but at some point, I'm certain that I crossed the five-minute mark. Eventually, time and embarrassment stopped being a factor and my motivation shifted solely to successfully chopping through the tree. I had to do this, there was no other choice. And eventually I did. As I picked up a piece of the pesky tree and celebrated my accomplishment, Bob came over with a few words of advice: "Just in case you cut wood next week or something, when you start out, don't go here, go here and here." Bob proceeded to breakdown the basics of wood chopping to me, specifically not to chop in a straight line, which he just watched me do for a decent amount of time without a peep. Instead, he waited for me to finish chopping with poor technique before providing guidance. All of this made sense with the next revelation.

Bob called me over to examine the ax closely and asked me to touch the sharp end. I was understandably apprehensive for fear of possibly cutting myself, but the result was far from a finger injury. The ax was dull as a butter knife, if not worse. Bob explained that he purposely does not sharpen the ax because that makes the chopping process harder. His preference is for wood chopping to be challenging and he consciously puts himself at a disadvantage with the "dullest ax in the world." I connected the dull ax to Bob watching me chop wood the wrong way and realized why he didn't provide his advice until after I had finished. My process was not about how to chop through the tree properly and skillfully, it was about the work and effort that went into it.

Consider how often in life you've taken the opportunity to make something easier for yourself. Advancements in many fields focus on minimizing human effort across the board, with one of the end results being the current sedentary lifestyle as the norm for many Americans. But what if we purposely made something harder? Are there benefits to hard work and effort, whether that be physical or mental? Or is it better to discover every advantage and short cut possible for the purpose of effort minimization? Let's revisit the concept of grit and see if research on this topic can provide us with further insight into another benefit of exercise.

Grit is a nuanced concept and deserves an entire book or several, which luckily are available if you want to learn more about this fascinating topic. In chapter one, I mentioned the work of psychologist Angela Duckworth, a subject matter expert on grit. She believes that there are two components to grit: perseverance and passion. Duckworth developed a grit scale that provides separate scores for both. It's worth taking to assess where you are with respect to your grit level. Duckworth's grit scale can be located at angeladuckworth.com/gritscale/.

Steven Kotler's work with peak performers led him to identify several components of grit: perseverance, willpower, mindset, passion, thought control, self-talk, gratitude, mindfulness, and the grit to master fear (2021). Since both Duckworth and Kotler identify perseverance as a key component of the grit formula, we'll focus on perseverance and tie it to high-intensity exercise.

But first, what is grit? The formal definition of grit is "courage and resolve; strength of character". Grit is the willingness to experience the discomfort necessary to move forward to achieve one's goals. It's the grunt work, the willingness to push through difficulties, and what the Navy Seals so eloquently term "embracing the suck." It's not only doing so occasionally but involves the day-to-day grind and persistence because you really care about what you are doing. Grit is understanding that certain paths do not have shortcuts. Grit is chopping wood with a dull ax on purpose.

Why is grit important? It may be one of the best predictors of success for human beings. Duckworth's research findings point to grit being more likely to predict academic success than IQ. Kotler points out that while grit "requires more energy and fortitude in the short run, it provides a much bigger boost in mood and motivation in the long run (p. 69)." Sometimes in life we overvalue immediate gratification and get lost in the pursuit of constant pleasure. The gritty path, even though not pleasant in the moment, leads to more happiness and well-being in the long run. Consider your own personal experiences where you accomplished something that was relatively easy versus something challenging. Which one of these accomplishments was more rewarding? Which one led to self-knowledge and growth? It's likely that the accomplishments which took more effort and perseverance were the ones that were ultimately more rewarding.

Think about when you exercise and the extent to which you challenge yourself every time you perform your activity of choice. On a scale of one to 10, how would you rate your intensity and level of exertion? Are you tapping into grit and specifically perseverance? Is what you are doing fun? I propose that HIT and HIIT are excellent ways to continuously challenge ourselves and a great path to train grit via physical exertion. With both training systems, you have the opportunity to push yourself outside of your comfort zone every single workout. The benefits are not only physical, but you may also tap into this important domain of grit building. If we can push ourselves physically on a regular basis, who says that we can't persevere in other aspects of our life? The grit we foster through intense training will come in handy as we take on different challenges and opportunities that come our way. Hard work is a necessary part of this process. Eventually we may develop the mindset where, as Bob Backlund proposes, we never capitulate.

Since You Now Know, the Choice Is Yours

There are countless exercise systems to choose from, yet the benefits of these systems vary. Some may even have a negative impact on the body over time due to an increased risk of injury or the continuous release of cortisol. Is there a point at which exercise is no longer a form of hormesis, or "good stress", and begins to cause more harm than good? I've laid out the argument for high-intensity training as an excellent exercise choice with many benefits, most importantly the building and maintenance of muscle which is imperative for a healthy and functional existence. High-intensity training provides the opportunity to significantly minimize the amount of time one spends in this self-care domain, which makes it easier to incorporate into everyday life. The trade-off is the brief discomfort when performing HIT, yet this may increase one's level of grit as one regularly pushes beyond their comfort zone. Considering the short time for exercise dosage, the motivation to train regularly may persist and eventually increase as progression of strength, shift in body composition and enhancement in energy levels pushes one to continue training. Incorporating HIIT provides the same exercise time reduction benefits as HIT while incorporating another effective training option with further health benefits.

Since we live in a society of convenience which conspires against our biology, with a food system driven by profit and not our health, and a medical system more reactive than proactive, it is ultimately and only up to us to take ownership of our health. Our level of self-care not only determines how we impact ourselves, but also affects our loved ones and society. There is ample compelling evidence that exercise provides significant health benefits when we incorporate it regularly into our lives. Now it's time to decide what form of movement will work best for you. Will it be a daily 30-minute walk? Will it be yoga, Pilates, or spin classes? Or will it be going to the gym several days a week for steady state aerobic or high-volume workouts? Or will it be high-intensity training? What are you willing to make time for to begin, and most importantly to continue exercise until it becomes a permanent part of your life?

There's No Ultimate Fitness

There is one more important point to consider when deciding on what exercise to choose: striving for continuously higher levels of fitness via exercise may eventually negatively impact health as health and fitness are not always synonymous. Hence, exercising more, which requires spending more time doing so, does not necessarily equate to better health. How so you may ask? One negative health consequence is the wear and tear on the body due to extensive exercise over many years. This tends to happen with running, and competitive sports where the participant performs the same mechanics repeatedly. Another issue is prolonged increased cortisol levels, as famous biohacker Dave Asprey experienced when he worked out six days a week for 90 minutes a day. Although he attained some benefits exercising so much, including strength, he did not lose the weight he was hoping to lose (Asprey 2014). Exercise is a form of stress and when overdone without the opportunity for proper recouperation, combined with a stressful job, it can end up not having the positive impact we hope for. Worst even, it can become a detriment to our health as increased cortisol levels tend to lead to weight gain and general burnout. As T.S. Wiley and Bent Formby point out in *Lights Out: Sleep, Sugar, and Survival*, an evolutionary perspective on health:

> The stress response enacted when you run for your life on that treadmill causes your cortisol levels to rise. If you do this once in a while, say every ten days, the natural episodic cortisol response will keep your heart and brain healthy. But if you exercise like a maniac more than once a week, the high cortisol levels resulting from all of the chronic exercise actually mimics the stress of mating season... (p. 14)

Hence, imagine thinking that you are doing something positive after a stressful day of work by going to the gym and exercising to de-stress, but you are conversely spiking your cortisol via excessive exercise at a time of the 24-hour cycle when it naturally decreases. Aside from exacerbating your health issues, this can lead to mounting frustration and eventual quitting of exercise altogether due to feeling poorly combined with a lack of results.

I would never dissuade anyone from doing something physical, considering our current collective health in this country, anything at this point is likely better than nothing. Yet, as you embark on your fitness journey, be mindful that balance is important. A 1984 article by Restak in the Washington Post discussed the concept of an "obligate runner – those for whom running is a compulsive drive that preempts fulfillment in other life areas or who run to the point of inflicting physical damage on their bodies." If you find yourself feeling quite upset or down when you miss a run or workout, you may likely be using exercise to fill a personal void. Exercise is just one vehicle for enhancing health and well-being, not the end all. Consider it something that provides us with the mental, physical, and energy enhancements to confidently go out into the world and find something that truly fulfills us.

The Final Verdict

For me, and many others around the world, HIT and HIIT are the ideal exercise vehicles for enhancement of health. Below is a general summary of the benefits:

1. Significantly minimize time spent exercising while still attaining muscle growth/maintenance and cardiovascular improvement.

2. Ease of incorporating into a daily schedule, which increases motivation to perform and maintain the behavior.

3. Regular opportunity to push outside one's comfort zone which may build/increase grit,

4. Look better and feel better.

5. All the health benefits associated with muscle.

6. Reducing the risk of disease.

7. Extremely safe which reduces risk of injury.

8. More time spent enjoying the benefits of exercise.

If you are like me, a parent and a full-time employee who has multiple responsibilities and does not want to invest significant time to exercise, or someone who doesn't want to spend hours in the gym every week, then high-intensity training is an excellent exercise option for you. There's discomfort involved but maybe Arthur Jones was right and there really shouldn't be anything pleasant about exercise if you are doing it right. Hunter-gatherers didn't run for their life or after food because it was a joyous experience. There is no easy path in any process of ascension, personal growth, or development. Even the slickest of body hacks or cheat codes require effort, with discomfort and difficulty likely a major part of the journey. The temporary, short discomfort associated with intense exercise is a fantastic alternative to golden years of chronic and debilitating pain associated with a life devoid of movement and self-care.

Chapter 5

Building Motivation To Exercise

An Afternoon at the Dorms

I sat in a chair looking around the bland room, rather unimpressed by my surroundings. Being a commuter, I missed out on the college campus experience that year, yet the aesthetics of this freshmen dorm made my home bedroom seem like a fantastic alternative. I raised the can of equally unimpressive beer to my mouth and took another sip. This was the last week of my freshmen year and the first time the two of us hung out alone for an extended amount of time. I knew that she liked me, and I liked her too. During that second semester of the school year, we were in a couple classes together and became friends. This afternoon was our first opportunity to become more, although our timing was not ideal considering the spring semester was about to end and we lived on opposite ends of the State.

We were talking and vibing as the conversation flowed and the beer began to take its effects. Then, out of nowhere, and with a gentle smile, the following words escaped her lips and pierced my soul: "You're...

sooo...skinny." This was an accurate description of me at the time and I was fully cognizant of my frail state due to the several mirrors in my house. I was also very conscious of and uncomfortable with my slim stature. Earlier that day, in preparation for hanging out with this young lady, I picked the perfect shirt which I thought enhanced my bony shoulders and made me look a bit bulkier than I was. To my dismay, this visual trickery failed miserably. The reality was, I weighed around 120 pounds on this day, and had gained exactly zero pounds and zero ounces since graduating high school.

As our day together continued, the s-word escaped her lips again. This one pierced even deeper than the first. I had been called skinny and other similar words throughout my life, by different people at different times. I felt each one of those comments but none of them had anywhere close to this impact. Whether it was the culmination of years of discomfort and insecurity with my body trumpeted in my face once again, or the fact that the observation came from someone who was a prospective romantic partner, this time it hit differently and it hit hard. It's fascinating how we can go for years in the framework of a certain reality, fully aware of our condition, a condition that may even have been verbalized here and there, without making any adjustments until that one day, that one situation, that one moment which finally tips the scale in the favor of change.

There is a wonderful quote by Anais Nin that I have on my wall in my home gym: "The day came when the risk to remain tight in a bud was more painful than the risk it took to blossom." This was going to be the last time someone called me skinny. I had a whole summer of free time ahead of me, a perfect opportunity to make some changes in my life and erase this sore spot in my psyche. I was 19-years old, soon to be 20, and still in danger of being blown away by a 40+ mph wind gust. It was time for me to blossom!!

I had dabbled with weight training here and there during my teenage years. A few friends had weight sets in their basements, where we would gather and bench press and curl because at that age, a massive chest and biceps was the only thing that mattered. Yet, I enhanced neither chest nor arms because these test-of-strength events were few and far in between. There was the one summer between 8th and 9th grade, when begrudgingly I agreed to join a small old-school gym at the insistence of my mom, who used the opportunity to hang out with her friend that lived next door to this muscle-making establishment. The gym was run by a former competitive bodybuilder and the patrons looked more like him than me. Even though everyone at the gym was very nice to me, it was beyond intimidating for a scrawny kid about to enter high school to spend 45 minutes to an hour among these gigantic, muscle-bound human beings. That summer wasn't my time yet, plus being skinny at that age was still par for course. I detested every time I had to step foot in that place and just went through the motions while doing my best to be invisible and not get in anyone's way. Little did I know then that weight training would one day become an integral part of my life.

You may be wondering how my day at the dorm concluded. It ended up being nothing more than a nice conversation with some flirting, a solid buzz from the substandard beer, plans for taking classes together the next semester, and a pleasant good-bye hug. We stayed in contact here and there during the summer, but nothing went beyond a friendship charged with mutual attraction. When we caught up at school the next semester, she was in the process of pledging for a sorority, which was a turnoff for me as I frowned down upon sororities and frats at that time in my life. Even though things never materialized on a deeper level, unbeknownst to her, this young lady and those three words had a massive impact on the direction of my life.

Discovering the Gym

I made the commitment to myself that the summer of 1998 would include joining a gym and staying consistent with training. Once school ended, I reached out to a good friend who was also finishing up his freshman year of college. Not only was my buddy Detrik finishing up a year of schooling but also his first year of college football. In stark contrast to me, Detrik stood at 5'10 and approximately 207 pounds of muscle. Out of all my friends, he was the one who could provide the best guidance when it came to working out and building some solid weight on my frail frame. I advised him of my plans to join a local gym for the summer and he agreed to join with me. Considering we also attained summer employment at the same place and worked the same afternoon to evening shift, we had every morning to spend at the gym. I cannot overstate how at this early stage of my change process, having a training partner kept me motivated and on track, especially one who really knew what he was doing. I was blessed with a friend and a personal trainer all in one.

Since 1998 was prior to the massive fitness club takeover, we had our choice of small, local old school gyms. Within a ten-mile radius, we had about four or five to choose from, and ended up going with Vinny's Iron Den, a refurbished garage with a couple extra rooms. The gym included no locker rooms, no towel service, whatever local radio station was playing, a hodge podge of random equipment brands, muscle magazines sprayed across the floors, a water fountain, and very hot summers. This was a no-nonsense gym! You may be wondering why the hot summers, gym's usually have walls, a roof, and central air. Vinny practiced electricity mindfulness. He would often open the garage door and turn on the standing fans throughout most of the morning and into the early afternoon before eventually turning on the air conditioning. Working up a sweat was unavoidable if you went to the gym early. This was a small inconvenience for us though.

That was it, 26 years ago, the beginning of my weight training journey. That first summer was a great learning experience. As with most weight training beginners, the initial quick gains in strength and slight muscle mass were great and kept me motivated – until I hit the plateau. Being inexperienced in resistance training and especially in eating for muscle gain, I had the misconception that I was going to continue to consistently and indefinitely gain five to 10 pounds on the bench press. That, of course, did not materialize and when it didn't, I responded with anger and frustration. Detrik had to go out of his way to ensure me that this is a normal part of the process. Unfortunately, for some, the plateau ends up being the end of their exercise journey. I thankfully still had my training buddy for another month to keep me motivated, accountable, and in the gym on a regular basis.

Once Detrik went back to college, I continued at Vinny's Iron Den for a couple more years. We had trained together for three months which was adequate time for me to learn the basics of resistance training, develop confidence when in the gym, feel better about the way I looked, and attain enough benefits in weight and muscle gain to continue with this new behavior. During the next couple years, I had two other short-term workout partners and eventually talked my girlfriend at the time into a membership. Vinny gave couples discounts anyways. As I continued to train, motivation shifted from "no longer wanting to be skinny" to liking how I looked in the mirror, the positive feedback I received from others regarding my physique, being more attractive to the opposite sex, and the continued increase in confidence and comfort in my own skin. These vanity-based reasons were my motivators for the first ten years of training, and still hold value to this day. Eventually, I was able to stack other motivators on top of this to make weight training a permanent part of my life. Before I explain that process, let's take a deeper look at building motivation for change and more importantly, how to maintain it long-term.

The Motivation to Change

Let's review the steps that led to the initial incorporation of resistance training into my life:

1. Years of unhappiness with the status quo, specifically how my body looked, which negatively impacted my confidence and self-esteem.

2. A very specific moment/situation that triggered the motivation for change, plus subsequent reflection to reach readiness for action.

3. A plan and the regularly scheduled time to incorporate the new behavior.

4. The support for proper learning and incorporating of the new behavior.

5. Benefits from the new behavior that further spurred motivation.

6. Positive reinforcement from self and others because of the new behavior.

In his book, *Why We Do What We Do: Understanding Self-Motivation*, professor of psychology and motivation subject matter expert Edward Deci stated,

> People's success at changing behavior begins with their taking genuine interest in their own motivations. This means asking themselves why they are trying to change, and thinking honestly about their answers. (p. 164)

Deci continued,

> The decision to change is one that individuals must make for themselves. That means exploring why they want to change and also paying attention to the benefits they are getting from the behavior. (p. 165)

The first big step in making a successful change is to figure out the why. Why would a 19-year-old begin resistance training? I'm confident my motivation was similar to that of most young men who start going to the gym – to look good and attract women. Period. It's that simple. I was tired of being the skinny guy and uncomfortable in my own skin. I lacked confidence and was extremely shy when it came to the opposite sex. I wanted to look in the mirror and feel good about myself. Bottom line, I was fed up with being who I was physically. To Deci's second point, the decision was absolutely mine and the benefits were ease to gauge, first with a quick increase in strength followed by a visible slight increase in muscle mass. This is usually what happens with underweight individuals who start weight training. For anyone who is overweight and resistance training to look and feel better about themselves, the assessment of benefits will likely be different and dietary interventions necessary. As we will see, vanity is a powerful motivator but if that's going to be the only driver of behavior, one needs to see those physical results.

As great as it is to finally get started with something new, building the motivation to incorporate a health-related behavior and the initial action-based follow-through are a small part of the process. This happens for a lot of people, specifically when gyms around the country fill up with new members on January 1st every year. By March and April though, most of these people are gone. They start off the year with a ton of momentum but due to several reasons, possibly not knowing what to do in the gym and getting bored with the treadmill, feelings of intimidation, lack of results and change in body, poor planning, and the colder months, the motivation wanes. Soon after, the old behavior patterns resurface until the next effort for change takes place.

When it comes to health and wellness, behavior change must be long-term for continued benefits, hence the phrase "lifestyle change." How do we not only build enough motivation to get started but develop motivation maintenance? One path is a deeper understanding of what motivates different aspects of ourselves, from the basic, to the rational, to the higher self. First, let's examine exercise and weight loss.

Exercise and Weight Loss

The health benefits of exercise are plentiful, but it's also important to examine what it may not be ideal for, which tends to be the main reason why people do it. Consider the next bit of this chapter controversial although there is evidence that maybe it shouldn't be. It is likely a fair assumption that most people, specifically in the United States of America, turn to exercise for weight loss. We have been sold on the eat less, move more strategy for weight loss for many years, to the point that it's rarely challenged. This strategy is supported by the medical community, by experts in the field of nutrition and exercise, and by the government, to the point where eat less, move more seems common sense. The backbone of this weight loss recommendation is the calorie in versus calorie out model. Taking the overwhelming support into consideration, why are so many people unsuccessful with weight loss long-term when they utilize this strategy?

There are many answers to this question. It may be that an individual is overemphasizing "burning calories" through step counting and treadmill use, then misjudging the amount of food consumed or turning food into a reward system, hence not creating the calorie deficit they were hoping to. Maybe they are over-exercising, raising cortisol in the process, and halting weight loss. Maybe the debunking of "aerobic" exercise as an effective strategy for weight loss is accurate. There is also the possibility of individual differences when it comes to exercise and appetite, which makes some people non-responders to exercise as a weight loss tool (Cox 2017). Or maybe exercise of any type is an ineffective path to weight loss and we should consider another model to explain why this may be the case.

An alternative theory to calorie in versus calorie out, or more properly termed as the "energy balance model", is the "carbohydrate insulin model", recently proposed by Gary Taubes in his book, *Good Calories, Bad Calories*. Further support for this model came from Dr. Jason Fung in *The Obesity Code, Unlocking the Secrets to Weight Loss*, as well as Dr. David Ludwig in *Always Hungry*. In these books, all three authors cited ample research which showed that exercise has minimal to no effect on weight loss. Taubes, Fung, and Ludwig pointed out that an increase in appetite caused by exercise elicits a response to eat more, which balances out the energy imbalance one is trying to achieve by moving more. They do support exercise for its other benefits, with Ludwig specifying improved insulin resistance and lowering of stress. Of course, there is still significant support for the "energy balance model", which includes research from Hall et al. (2022) that presents a more accurate description of the "energy balance model." There are also research findings that support exercise as a weight loss strategy, but they involved the subjects exercising excessively and beyond the CDC recommendation for health (Cox 2017). Considering the high failure rate of people who utilize exercise for weight loss combined with conflicting research, should the motivation to exercise be driven by weight loss goals?

There are plenty of other amazing exercise-related benefits, specifically from resistance training, as outlined in the prior chapter. Refocusing our reasons and motivation to exercise based on the definitive health benefits such as increases in functionality, life span, health span, and all other benefits that come with muscle, is a step in the right direction. Still, this rational approach may not be strong enough of a motivator for everyone to turn exercise into a long-term behavior. If the goal is weight loss alone, and we do not see the results we are expecting, it is very likely that motivation will wane, and we may not continue with regular physical activity. Unfortunately, the scale is too often the sole measurement of progress and assessment as to the impact of exercise. Should we instead use other measurable outcomes, such as body composition gauged via measuring tape, a body fat monitor, or simply how we fit in our clothes? A 2021 systematic review and meta-analysis of the effects of resistance training found that this form of exercise reduced body fat percentage, body fat mass, and visceral fat in healthy adults (Wewege et al.). Connecting our exercise efforts, specifically resistance training, to improved body composition is more likely to lead to success. It may also tap into the deeper need to look and feel good.

Another reason not to hyperfocus on weight loss when embarking on an exercise program is that fitness and thinness do not always go hand in hand. It is possible to be fit while carrying excess weight. Individuals who overly focus on weight loss through exercise may end up cutting a very effective training program short because the fitness enhancement is not easily detectable and visible in the mirror nor the scale. Per Gibala in *The One-Minute Workout*, fitness is a greater predictor of mortality rates and chronic disease than weight. Normal weight people who are unfit may have more to worry about when it comes to health than fit people with a high body mass index (BMI). Again though, are fitness and lowering one's risk for chronic disease and early death, adequate motivators if one is still overweight? For some, this may be the case. We also must consider the social stigma associated with carrying excess weight. Ultimately, if motivation to exercise is connected to the need to look and feel better and losing weight is a must for the individual, a dietary intervention will be necessary for truly visible results.

Motivation Maintenance

At this point in my life, not exercising is not an option. I've outlined what led to the behavior change and the motivation that drove my continuation of resistance training for the initial decade of training. Not until I reached my 30s, did I begin considering the health benefits of exercise, and not till my 40s did I truly connect to the bigger picture of how my behavior can positively impact others. Over 26 years, I've managed to tap into motivational factors connected to the different aspects of the self, aspects that are part of us all. These are the Basic Self, Conscious Self, and the Higher Self, as described by prolific author, lecturer, and spiritual leader Dan Millman in his book, *No Ordinary Moments*.

If these three selves were to verbalize why I continue to exercise regularly, they would say the following:

> *Basic Self* – "I really like how I look in the mirror. I can still wear tight clothes and look good in them, and I really like when others tell me that I look good for my age. Having well defined muscles in my 40s and looking fit – it really feels good! And I like going out and being around others."
>
> *Conscious Self* – "Exercise is good for my health and well-being, it helps me lessen stress, have energy all day long, more balance, functionality, prevents illness, and is likely to extend my health-span for many years."
>
> *Higher Self* – "I can really be an inspiration to others through exercise, support them, and show that at any age we are capable of anything. Exercise is my vehicle for enhancing others' lives."

Millman explains the Basic Self as your subconscious, the inner child. Like all children, it thrives on fun, play, and pleasure, as well as power and success. The Conscious Self, or ego, is your reason and logic, the guide for rational decision-making. The Higher Self, or spiritual self, is your ultimate potential, your greater impact in the service of others. We'll use Millman's model to assess how motivation to exercise can be maintained over time. Let's begin with the Basic Self.

The Basic Self

Men's Health "Gym and Fridge" is a YouTube program in which *Men's Health Magazine* visits celebrities and explores their refrigerators and gyms to assess what they eat and how they exercise. In the summer of 2023, they interviewed 74-year-old professional wrestling legend, Ric Flair. During the gym portion of the interview, Ric was asked what keeps him motivated to exercise regularly; his answer was one word and he said it four times – "Vanity". That's it. He did not mention health, longevity, mobility, nor enhanced intelligence. Flair also provided very specific exercise goals for the day he turns 75, which likely further enhanced his motivation to exercise. Dan Millman shares a story in *No Ordinary Moments* regarding the motivation that pushed him to train as a competitive gymnast and eventual champion when he was in college. He pushed himself daily, often to the point of complete exhaustion "to gain recognition, admiration, and adulation; I believed my gymnastics prowess would make me more attractive to women (p. 91)." As I mentioned already, these are the same underlying motives that pushed me to exercise regularly for the first ten years and hold significant value to this day. Although not something that people tend to brag about or even admit, these are the energies of the Basic Self. Outside of looking and feeling good about oneself, this part of us also thrives on excitement, pleasure, and if in a bad situation, will seek out the lesser pain.

The Conscious Self

Everything I outlined in the health benefits of exercise chapter, is connected to the Conscious Self. This logical and reasonable part of us takes into consideration that regular exercise will greatly minimize illness and enhance our health. It will give us more energy, and increase mobility, fitness, longevity, intelligence, and our health span. We all know that the benefits of exercise are phenomenal, so why isn't everyone doing it? Why is it that the minority of the United States population have made exercise a life-long journey? Because the Conscious Self alone likely does not have adequate motivational energy to get people started, let alone continue with exercise long-term. Logic is great but it's not a major motivational tool. This may be the reason why continuous warnings from doctors during yearly check-ups advising patients that they need to start exercising or things will get worst, are not adequate motivators for action, even if the patient fully understands the situation. "Yes, I'm overweight and my bloodwork is not trending in the right direction, I know I should exercise to get these numbers right." It makes perfect sense too but long-term follow through on the obvious tends to be the exception. Sometimes significant events such as type-2 diabetes diagnoses or even a heart attack is not adequate for behavior change. As Millman points out, the Conscious Self needs to get the Basic Self onboard to spark the excitement for action. More on this process soon.

The Higher Self

The Higher Self as a motivational energy is not often connected to exercise, although I do believe it can serve as a behavioral driver if one notices the opportunity. Such a chance presents itself when an individual makes significant, positive strides with their physiques. I remember two specific health coaching clients of mine who made phenomenal short-term physical progress with a combination of dietary changes (not dieting) and resistance exercise, plus running. Their bodies changed so drastically, friends and acquaintances approached them to ask how they did it and for health advice. These two men became embodiments of change for the better. This was the opening to tap into motivation via the Higher Self through service to others. Sometimes the results of our behaviors are bigger than us and can positively impact the people around us. Once we realize this, we can use the motivation to inspire others as a reason for continuing with exercise. This is one of my drivers. Further ways to tap into motivation through the Higher Self include a connection to the understanding that taking care of our bodies through exercise is a representation of self-love, and that physical discomfort can serve as a gateway to greater illumination and self-knowledge.

Getting the Basic Self Onboard

Millman points out in his work that the energy of the Basic Self is needed for behavior change. It also holds great value in the maintenance of a positive behavior long-term. How do we get the Basic Self onboard? One path Millman recommends is vivid visualization, a technique that athletes have used for many years for successful outcomes (Hall 2001). Outside of the realm of sports, visualization has proven beneficial in academics (Vasquez & Buehler 2007) and employment (Neck & Manz 1992). Considering that the Basic Self thrives on excitement, fun, and pleasure, our visualization needs to connect the benefits of exercise to these results. What vivid imagery comes with seeing ourselves enjoying life, vibrant, having fun, feeling good about ourselves, being liked by others, and being successful in life? What do we look like thriving daily and at our absolute best and what will we be able to accomplish after we make exercise a regular part of our life? The specific imagery will likely differ for everyone, depending on what excites each of our Basic Selves. Millman also points out that there are benefits to visualizing the negative aspects of staying as is, considering the Basic Self seeks pleasure and avoids pain. Not exercising may include imagery connected to tiredness, poor performance, not looking or feeling good, etc. Another option is giving ourselves rewards for exercising, a process used in habit-building. Reward choices should not negate the effort that went into exercising, as in eating half of a pizza following a workout, but instead could be a massage, small purchase, relaxing bath, or an exciting activity – something that is pleasurable and associated with the change.

Motivation through the three selves is not relegated to exercise only, it is applicable to any behavior change process. Whatever we attempt to do, gaining the energy of the Basic Self holds the most value, as Millman points out:

> If we decide to achieve something, if we associate that change with a sense of security or fun or personal power, the Basic Self will give us the energy to accomplish the task, because it wants the carrot. If the goal has little to do with these three things, we probably won't persist. (p. 92)

In the continued progression of writing this book, the Basic Self has been along for the entire ride. Yes, the overarching drivers are to inspire, to help, and to provide insight into self-care to those who read this book, in hopes of making their life better. But I would be lying to you if the thoughts of recognition from others didn't cross my mind. To attain energy from the Basic Self I sometimes visualize the book release party, everyone that is going to be there to support me, all the fun that we'll have, and the great speech that I'll give.

The Logistics of HIT and HIIT Aid Motivation Too

The duration of exercise can greatly impact motivation as well. Considering that one of the main reasons people provide as to why they don't exercise is a lack of time, if we significantly negate the time it takes to exercise, as both HIT and HIIT do, then the likelihood of incorporating and maintaining this behavior will increase. Programs like Fit20 and The Perfect Workout both provide the opportunity for building, increasing, and maintaining motivation in several ways:

1. Short workout negating the "not having time" reason.
2. Personal trainer to track progress, support, and maintain accountability.

3. Scheduled appointments to further negate time and easily fit the workout into one's life.
4. Strength and muscle gains.

The familiarity of the workout helps as well. Every time a member comes in for a training session, they know exactly what they will do, but can still challenge themselves to push harder through the machine exercises.

We can tap into those four motivational factors without joining either program. High-intensity training can be performed without a personal trainer, instead a gym partner can provide support and accountability. One can also track his or her progress using a journal or app. Ideally, we develop a regular time to go to the gym each week within our schedule, and if you train using HIT, it'll likely only be one or two gym visits a week. Lastly, the workouts will still be short, and the benefits will come because this way of exercise works.

In *Body by Science*, McGuff and Little introduce a 12-minute per week resistance training exercise regimen. Fit20 increases the timeframe to 20 minutes per week with a similar machine-based system. My home workouts total approximately 60 minutes per week, with breaks. Schoenfeld et al. (2019) concluded that:

> ...marked increases in strength can be attained by resistance trained individuals with just three 13-minute sessions per week, and that gains are similar to that achieved with a substantially greater time commitment when training in a moderate loading range (eight to 12 repetitions per set) (p. 102).

The researchers further state that "this finding has important implications for those who are time-pressed, allowing the ability to get stronger in an efficient manner, and may help to promote greater exercise adherence in the general public" (p. 102). Whether it's 12, 20, 39, or 60 minutes, these are minimal weekly time obligations for what I consider a non-negotiable behavior. Most importantly, by incorporating resistance training into your life, you're likely to look better, feel better, and function better every single day.

Effective Efficiency and Motivation

HIT and HIIT are great ways to exercise, but you would not know unless something spurred you internally to try one, the other, or both. First, adequate motivation is necessary to start with any behavior change, but then and most important, is the motivation maintenance to continue with the behavior long term, especially within the realm of health and wellness. A rational approach to incorporating exercise in one's life may be adequate to get things moving, but likely not enough to continue long-term. Motivational support is needed from a deeper place, connecting our behavior outcomes to excitement, fun, and pleasure, to ensure that exercise is going to be a long-term lifestyle change. For some, motivation will also come from a more purposeful place, one which takes into consideration the journey of self-knowledge as well as how our behavior can positively impact others. Further motivation comes from logistical strategies such as the short amount of time needed to dedicate to HIT and HIIT, creating a set schedule for exercise, and ideally having a support and accountability system, whether that be a personal trainer, workout partner, or becoming a member of a community dedicated to exercise and self-care. Lastly, seeing the benefits of these exercise strategies, whether that be strength and muscle gain, fitting better in clothes, or enhanced functionality and movement, will be further motivation to continue with the behavior. At the end of the day, everyone wants to look and feel good about themselves, which are likely to be the most powerful drivers for life-long exercise.

There is one overarching thought that keeps me fully committed to exercise and the other forms of self-care I've incorporated long-term: "I want to be at 100% every single day." This requires a steady flow of energy from when I begin my day in the morning to when I unwind at night. Outside of steady energy levels, being at 100% includes high levels of focus, mental clarity, mental sharpness, wit, confidence, stamina, and a general feel good. Everyone I interact with every day deserves my best. My family in the morning when I prep my kids for school, my co-workers, friends, and again my family when I get home after work. Of course, there will be days when my sleep is off, when I don't eat well, or when I just feel like crap, but the drive is still there to be at my best seven days a week. Exercise is a big part of this process, but it must be effectively efficient so that I spend as little time as possible doing it while maximizing my time with family, friends, and projects like writing this book.

Chapter 6

One Man's Food Journey

Several times each day, we decide on how to nourish our bodies. Sometimes the decision is conscious and deliberate, sometimes it involves little to no thought, and sometimes it may be driven by cravings and other factors. These decisions impact how we feel that day, ranging from sluggish and fatigued, to energetic and lively, or somewhere in between. What we eat determines whether we experience a midday energy crash or coast through the day fully turbo charged. Aside from this daily impact of food, there are long-term consequences, with obesity and related disease at the problematic end of the spectrum. Food matters - a lot.

Considering food's impact on our health, both short and long-term, what should we eat, that will provide our bodies with the nutrients necessary to not only boost daily energy levels, but greatly enhance the likelihood of a disease-free life? What foods should we avoid? How do we navigate a food system that is profit-driven with little to no care for the health outcomes of the consumer? After answering these questions, we must take the next step of figuring out how to prep and cook the food that will benefit us the most, in the fastest time possible. How do we become effectively efficient in the kitchen?

Food Relations

For the first thirty years of my life, food quality and nutrition were unexplored topics of discussion or contemplation in my household. Food was simply . . . food. My first nine years on earth were spent in Poland and upon immigration to the United States in late 1987, I seamlessly integrated into American food culture with zero thought as to what I was eating. And what nine-year-old transitioning from post-Communist Poland would dare find fault with such an array of enticing edible goods? "Oh, hi there, extremely colorful box of colorful loops with a random happy cartoon character on it, I've never seen you before. And what is this inside – a toy! Who puts toys in food? A darn genius!" I was quickly charmed by the glitz and glamour of processed food. And bananas, copious amounts of bananas because those were not available in the "old country", although I did tire of the bananas rather quickly. Thankfully there was a counterbalance to the processed food I was immersed in, that being traditional home-cooked meals, a part of the culture that immigrant families tend to bring to the land of opportunity. My grandfather was a cook by profession, but grandma was the one who did all the home cooking. My mom also cooked, hence there were always home cooked meals prepped for me during my formative years.

Mom continued to cook daily well into my 20s, although the food slowly morphed into American-like fare. Aside from the home cooking, for years it was the token cereal and orange juice in the morning, massive, processed meat filled sandwiches and sugar-laden tasty snack cakes for lunch, and whatever else was on hand. The cupboards were always filled with chips, sweets, random heavily processed snacks, soda, and regularly scheduled ice cream in the freezer. I also ate an awe-inspiring number of hot dogs during my teenage years – predominantly for breakfast (yes, I know – yuk!). Aside from the home cooking, there were the obligatory pizza nights, chicken nights, Chinese food nights, and countless visits to the local Burger King, Wendy's, and McDonalds. I went about consuming all of this food without a thought as to its impact on my body. I had no clue what organic was, nor pasture-raised, wild-caught, sustainable-sourced, or any other quality-elevating description. Food was food and I ate what was available when I was hungry. There was no one in my family nor a formal nutrition education component at my school to advise me that prolonged consumption of this sort of stuff may eventually lead to health complications later in life.

Around my mid-20s, I began developing a basic awareness of food's impact on the body. At the same time, considering that I was weight training almost daily, I reckoned I could exercise my way out of eating wantonly, hence I continued eating anything and everything. This was also around the time that I certified as a personal trainer and got a side gig at a local Gold's Gym. A deeper interest in exercise and the human body spurred an interest in nutrition. This peaked in my early 30s, when I enrolled in a health coaching certification program in New York City. The program was more inspirational than educational, and I had the pleasure of listening to some of the champions of nutrition and other forms of self-care, in-person every weekend. Watching live presentations from the likes of Walter Willett, Mark Hyman, Andrew Weil, Bernie Siegel, and Marion Nestle was truly inspiring. Seeing raw foodist David Wolfe put approximately twenty ingredients in a Vitamix and blend it into a palatable concoction was pure mind blown! The school did a great job of bringing in speakers who presented different dietary perspectives. A lot of the information was new to me – I did not know what the heck kale or quinoa was prior to the first day of class. There was one very clear take-home – what you eat absolutely matters when it comes to health. Most people are aware of this but in a food system that is contradictory, convoluted, and engulfed in processed stuff masquerading as sustenance, it can be difficult to properly act on the awareness. How do we get to the point of conscious eating – a place where we can smoothly navigate the intricacies of the good, the bad, and the "is this even food?" For me, that process started with formal education and continued through self-educating. I soaked all the information up like a sponge and began incorporating the things that I learned into my daily diet. Conscious, guilt-free healthy eating developed through this process.

My health coaching education provided the dietary guidance that should have been available in some capacity earlier in my life through formal education. Unfortunately, outside of a general overview of the food pyramid in health class, nutrition education was completely missing in the schools I attended in the 90s – a big miss by the local education system. Considering the obesity epidemic started taking off in the late 70s, with accompanying health issues and significant impacts on many levels of society, a more thorough nutrition component in academia during my time in grade and high school in the 90s would have been beneficial. Even if the information at that time no longer holds value and was debatable to begin with, this educational component may have at the least assisted me and many other teenagers at that time who were indiscriminately eating anything and everything, with some level of understanding of how food impacts the body and possibly led to a more mindful consumption.

I lucked out in that my interests and curiosity, and eventually passion, ended up in the health realm. I have a feeling not too many people read nutrition books for pleasure, but I do. As informative and exciting as the content of these books can be, if you read enough of them, it will become very clear why nutrition has become such a confusing topic. One expert says this food is good for you, another says it's not but eat this instead, a third says that neither of those foods are healthy, and a fourth contradicts the first three with a completely new take the topic. From plant-based, to keto, to microbiome-focused, to meat-based, low carb, low fat, fasting, micronutrient, and everything in between, are there general commonalities that these doctors, researchers, and scientists can all agree on when it comes to food and nutrition? That is what we'll attempt to determine in this and the next chapter, and once we figure out what to eat and what to avoid, I'll provide examples of effectively efficient healthy meals that can be prepped rather quickly. You'll also read stories about real people who significantly enhanced their health and lost a lot of weight through interventions that excluded exercise. Before we get to all that though, it's important to understand that genetics matter.

Genetics Matter When It Comes to Weight

One of the results of the Standard American Diet, with the highly appropriate SAD acronym, is weight gain and obesity. The rates of obesity in the United States have steadily climbed since the 1970s and sat at 41.9% in 2023 per a report from Trust for America's Health. Linked directly to obesity are type-2 diabetes, coronary heart disease, stroke, high blood pressure, sleep apnea, pain, low functionality, and a general low quality of life. Our food system does not support the resolution of these health issues, but instead exasperates them. Also important to understand is that even if an individual's body max index (BMI) does not place them in the obese category, that does not mean this person can mindlessly consume copious amounts of SAD – the lifestyle diseases associated with obesity may also impact individuals who do not gain weight so readily.

Genetics are sometimes overlooked or not given adequate attention when it comes to weight gain and the subsequent health consequences. In the earlier mentioned book, *The Obesity Code*, Dr. Jason Fung states that "70 percent of your tendency to gain weight is determined by your parentage. Obesity is overwhelmingly inherited" (p. 24). In their research, Masood and Moorthy (2023) point out that the estimated heritability of obesity is between 40 and 70 percent. What does that look like for you? It's sobering to consider that the genetic cards we are dealt hold significant value when it comes to our propensity for gaining weight, but being cognizant of this reality is necessary so that our health strategies are appropriate, realistic, and personalized. It's important to be truthful with ourselves when assessing genetic hurdles on the path towards health. For some, the health journey may be a more arduous process than it is for others, depending on genetics and where one is when they begin said journey. Of equal importance is the understanding that even though we may be predisposed to weight gain, our lifestyle and dietary decisions hold great value in the ultimate outcome (Masood & Moorthy 2023).

From an evolutionary perspective regarding human propensity for weight gain, there are competing theories as to whether we are predisposed for weight gain or leanness. If the human body indeed evolved to gain weight, this held significant benefits when there was plenty to eat, specifically an excess in carbohydrates, in the summer and little to eat in the winter. Whatever fat we stored during the bountiful warm seasons and the accompanying metabolic changes, including insulin resistance, were a deciding factor for our survival through the cold months. Hence, the propensity to gain weight was an evolutionary necessity (Wiley 2000). The other perspective states that humans did not necessarily hibernate hence there would be no benefit from gaining significant amounts of weight in the summer to prep for the winter and that societies existed where food was plentiful year-round – therefore, evolution favors leanness, not obesity (Fung 2016). Whichever side you prefer, the reality is that obesity and the diseases it's linked to have not existed at the rate they've hit beginning in the 1970s. Genetics alone cannot explain the profound increase in overweight and obesity rates over the past 50 years in this country. Something environmental triggered this, but is there concurrence regarding the culprits?

Governmental Guidance on Sugar Intake

The 2020-2025 Dietary Guidelines for Americans advise to "limit foods and beverages higher in added sugars" with added sugars being "less than 10% of calories per day starting at age two." Furthermore, in recent years our government has incorporated an "added sugar" category to food labels with a percent daily value to provide consumers with perspective on their daily intake. For example, a serving size of Rice Krispies contains four grams of added sugar which constitutes eight percent of the recommended daily intake. The Rice Krispies do have a not so confounding variable, which is the 30 or so grams of processed carbohydrate from rice per serving. Hence, the focus on added sugar is a step in the right direction but one must also consider the processed, easily digestible carbohydrates when choosing what they are going to eat.

Suggesting that Americans should incorporate less than 10% of calories per day of added sugar starting at age two assumes that most Americans have an in-depth understanding about the percentages of their daily caloric intake, which is not the case. The American Heart Association provides clearer guidance regarding added sugar, specifically 36 grams or nine teaspoons a day for men and 25 grams or six teaspoons a day for women. These exact numbers may increase the chances of adherence as it's easier to count grams on food labels versus tracking a specific percentage of daily caloric intake. The Dietary Guidelines do provide a chart on page 36 titled "Beverages and Added Sugar" which displays names of beverages, including conversions from calories to grams, to teaspoons for each. The daily consumption of processed foods, such as sweetened beverages, sweet snacks, candy, and dessert, makes it easy to hit and go above both the AHA and USDA recommendations.

The United States has made strides with their food guidelines since the original guidance in the 1970s. Interestingly, those initial efforts coincided with the beginning of the obesity epidemic. In 1977, Senator George McGovern introduced the country to the Dietary Goals for the United States to address the rise in chronic disease. These goals recommended a reduction in dietary fat consumption, although the quality of the science behind this recommendation was conspicuous (Taubes 2007). Whether Americans succeeded in lessening the amount of fat in their diets is up for debate (Taubes 2007; Temple 2022). We do know that food companies introduced ample fat-free processed food options into the grocery stores, often replacing the fat with processed carbohydrate such as high fructose corn syrup. In 1992, the Food Pyramid was introduced, the base of which held a recommendation for six to 11 servings of bread, cereal, rice, and pasta each day. Lobbying factored into the creation of the pyramid (Nestle 2002). The pyramid's apex recommended that added sugars be used sparingly. So, what where the outcomes of the pyramid and dietary recommendations? Per data from Temple's (2022) paper, "the prevalence of obesity in American adults (age 20–74, both genders) rose from 15.0% in 1976–1980, to 23.3% in 1988–1994, and to 30.9% in 1999–2000 (p. 1)." What caused this steady increase in obesity? Was it faulty recommendations, lobbying, fat, carbohydrate, lack of exercise, sugar, processed food, or something else?

Likely Causes of the Obesity Epidemic

As difficult as it seems for nutrition experts to agree on what people should eat, it's a much easier lift to provide guidance on things that people should not consume. That agreement lands squarely on the shoulders of sugar as its intake increased in proportion to the obesity epidemic. One of the main vehicles for the extra sugar in our diet were, and still are, sugar-sweetened beverages. In any attempt to shift one's diet towards a healthy lifestyle, it's prudent to greatly minimize the consumption of sugar-laden foods, along with other simple and refined carbohydrates. Did fat intake increase in proportion to the rise of obesity? Interestingly, Temple's (2022) review of the origins of the obesity epidemic determined that dietary fat made a trivial impact if that. He further points out: "it is unlikely that a decrease in physical activity played a significant role in the epidemic" (p. 2). Outside of sugar, what other factors impacted Americans' health negatively starting around the 1970s, and more importantly, which of these can we control?

Out of consumers control were the farm bills which increased farmer subsidies, that may have led to excess agricultural products that were then turned into cheap, "ultra-processed food" (Temple 2022). That cheap, processed food continues to take up space in most supermarkets, predominantly in the middle of each store. Guidance for healthy food shopping often includes ensuring that one purchases much of their food from around the stores' perimeter. Since processed food is cheaper, people are more likely to buy it. This is where socioeconomic status comes into play, specifically the reality that not everyone can afford the more expensive food that comprises healthier diets. Taubes (2007), among others, pointed out the connection between poverty and obesity. This is an unfortunate reality that needs to be addressed through government-driven policies so that every American can have access to affordable, healthy food options.

Culprit #2 - Processed Foods

The increase in consumption of processed food factored in the rise of obesity as well. If one possesses the spending flexibility to pick between processed foods and healthier options, such as organic vegetables, fruits, nuts, and quality sources of protein, choosing the latter will enhance positive health outcomes. There is one more factor to consider – fast food restaurants. In their systematic review, Nago et al. (2014) concluded that "eating out-of-home frequently, in the broad sense, is positively associated with the risk of becoming overweight or obese and weight change" (p. 1103). Hence, the importance of controlling our ingredients via home cooked meals. Since the choice to consume processed and fast food is partially driven by convenience, home cooking alternatives that are quick and easy to make are necessary. In the next chapter we'll review a few homecooked meals that are effectively efficient. The self-experiment in the appendix provides examples of pre-made snack foods that possess nutritional value.

Ultimately, outside of future government policies impacting the sale and availability of processed foods, which some would deem wishful thinking, it is up to us, the ones who make the daily choice as to how we feed ourselves and our families, to focus our spending dollar away from processed foods. Every time you enter your local supermarket, you decide what's going to be on the shelves with your purchases. There have already been significant shifts in the availability of healthier food options, as anyone who's food shopped during the past 20 years can see. Hopefully, as more people connect the food they eat to how they look and feel, their energy levels, and long-term health, the market will shift towards more healthy options with lower price tags on them.

Food Label Guidance

When purchasing foods with labels, a quick scan of the label for total grams of sugar, as well as total carbohydrate, is a worthy endeavor. There are a lot of "health foods" on shelves which contain significant amounts of sugar. One example is pre-made beverages that tout significant amounts of vegetables and fruit in each bottle, yet a quick glance at the label displays anywhere from 30 to 50 grams of sugar, with no fiber in sight. Just because something says "100% real juice" in massive letters on the front of the bottle does not mean that this is a healthy option. Outside of reading labels for the ingredient list, which ideally you choose foods with the least ingredients, this quick glance at the sugar content may be the deciding factor as to whether you put what's in the container into your body. As mentioned earlier, four grams of sugar equals one teaspoon. When reading a food label for sugar content, make that calculation in your head and then imagine pouring that many teaspoons of sugar into the bottle you're holding. Lastly, stay away from zero-calorie sugar alternatives as they raise insulin as well and do not lead to weight loss nor have any health benefits.

Chapter 7

Nutrition Concensus

Expert Perspectives on Sugar and Carbohydrates

As mentioned already, one aspect of the American diet that increased in proportion with the rise of the obesity epidemic was sugar intake, specifically in the form of sugar sweetened beverages (Temple 2022). Yet, the totality of simple and refined carbohydrates needs to be addressed. Dr. Joel Fuhrman, a proponent of a nutrient-rich, plant-based diet states in his book, *Eat to Live*, that "almost all weight-loss authorities agree on this – you must cut out the refined carbohydrates, including bagels, pasta, and bread" (p. 39). Yes, these are the same foods that formed the base of the original food pyramid. Other examples of refined and simple carbohydrates include white rice, pizza, pastries, breakfast cereals, candy, and fruit juice. Dr. David Ludwig, who's dietary recommendations focus on the importance of fat and protein, discusses in his work, *Always Hungry?*, the impact of the rate of absorption of fructose, which is a component of sugar, high fructose corn syrup, and other sweeteners. He states that there has been a significant increase in fructose consumption since the 70s, which is another dietary variable that coincides with the onset of the obesity epidemic. Fructose is metabolized in the liver and considering the workload that the liver has outside of processing excessive amounts of fructose daily, health issues may occur over time, specifically fatty liver. Fatty liver is associated with other health problems such as insulin resistance, high blood pressure, and high triglycerides, which are intimately connected to type-2 diabetes, strokes, heart disease, and Alzheimer's (Ludwig 2016).

It's imperative that we are aware of the physiological mechanisms in play and how things go awry over time with regular consumption of sugar and other refined and simple carbs. When we consume a food with sugar (comprised of glucose and fructose), a soda for example, the body responds by addressing the quick increase of glucose in the blood by releasing insulin, which drives the sugar into cells. The glucose is used for energy or stored as fat. As mentioned, the fructose is metabolized by the liver. Many years of this process results in the cells becoming resistant to insulin, as the body continues to store fat over time, likely leading to weight gain. To add insult to injury, our appetite remains strong and the body cannot utilize the stored fat in the adipose tissue for energy with a steady, carb-heavy diet. Once the weight is on, the longer someone maintains a state of obesity, the more difficult it is to reverse the matter.

Doctors Elizabeth Blackburn and Elissa Epel are subject matter experts on the topic of telomeres. In their book, *The Telomere Effect*, they explain that telomeres are the "repeating segments of noncoding DNA that live at the ends of your chromosomes. Telomeres, which shorten with each cell division, help determine how fast your cells age and when they die, depending on how quickly they wear down (p. 6)." Blackburn's and Epel's incredible findings focus on the reality that the ends of the chromosomes can actually lengthen, which greatly impacts the reality of aging, specifically how we age. Getting chronologically older doesn't necessarily have to result in progressive deterioration and decay. As you can probably guess, sugar and other simple carbohydrates are associated with shorter telomeres. From their perspective, the delivery method matters, which is the "fast rush of sugar with no fiber to slow it down (p. 234)."

Doctor David Perlmutter is a subject matter expert on gut bacteria, or the microbiome, and how this amazing internal system impacts our health. The microbiome is intimately connected to many, if not all, aspects of our health and well-being. Ideally, it is diverse with "good bacteria." A less diverse microbiome, sometimes called a Westernized gut microbiome, and/or one overrun by "bad bacteria" is associated with chronic disease. In his work, *Brain Maker*, Perlmutter discusses the impact of fructose on the microbiome, calling fructose "one of the most insidious villains". As we've seen with other examples of fructose's negative impact, Perlmutter points out the overload on the liver, which as stated before is the organ that must deal with the excess fructose. In the process of metabolizing fructose, the liver's production of other hormones, such as leptin, is compromised. Leptin is involved in the suppression of appetite; hence fructose negatively impacts our hunger cues. Furthermore, fructose feeds "pathogenic gut bacteria, thereby disrupting a healthy microbial balance (p. 111)."

You may be wondering about the fructose in fruit. Fruit is a source of fructose, although also possesses fiber that slows down the absorption of sugars. Fruit also contains vitamins and antioxidants that positively impact our health. Fruits vary in their nutritional value with general agreement that berries are the cream of the crop, considering their high nutrient profile and low sugar content. At the end of the day, if someone is going to transition from consuming copious amounts of high fructose corn syrup and other processed sugar to daily intake of fruit, that's a win. If my health coaching client has been consuming a muffin daily for breakfast and we successfully transition to an apple instead, that's progress. One can debate the impact of fruit, but often a person's current dietary standard is the determining factor as to whether the consumption of fruit or any other debatable food is a step in the right direction.

We've explored the issues with sugar, other easily digestible carbohydrates, and processed foods from several different angles with the conclusion being, going back to the USDAs recommendation, that these foods need to be greatly minimized. One important factor that we've not addressed yet is that sugar impacts the same pleasure receptors in the brain as addictive substances. As David Ludwig points out in *Always Hungry?*:

> When the bloodstream runs low on calories, the brain triggers an alarm system, leading to hunger, and cravings. We specifically crave highly processed carbohydrates – chips, cookies, crackers, candy, cake and the like – for one simple reason: They make us feel better within a few minutes. The problem is, they make us feel worse for hours afterward, setting up the next addictive cycle. In a sense, highly processed carbohydrates are akin to drugs of abuse, whose fast absorption rates increase addictiveness. (p. 61)

From an evolutionary perspective, Wiley and Formby point out another trigger for carbohydrate consumption in their book, *Lights Out*, that being excessive light, specifically artificial light at nighttime. This light exposure, which has only been around for 100 years, tricks the body into thinking it's the long days of summer, meaning "that your brain will force you to seek energy for storage by eating sugar (p. 13). Even though sugar cravings are a real thing that a lot of us can relate to, with a slew of triggers, a 2016 perspective article reviewing the science of sugar addiction did not find adequate support for including it into public policy recommendations (Westwater et al.). Nevertheless, the human body is not equipped to handle the current rate of sugar consumption and strategies are needed to address this concern.

Addressing Sugar Intake

Some people will go through their entire lives never connecting how the food they eat impacts their health. Even dire warnings from doctors, with end results such as amputations or blindness due to type-2 diabetes complications, are not adequate of a stimulus for behavior modification.

The insidiousness of this whole process is that it takes many, many years of sugar and refined carbohydrate consumption to reach the point of a disease state. By then, the eating behavior is well ingrained, driven by the underlying biological factors. Furthermore, the effects of the metabolic issues may not be acute enough to provide significant physical cues that would aid in halting the behavior. This deterioration of health is a slow and steady process, plus medical science has created interventions to buffer some of the negative impacts, extending our diseased state of life. At what point does an individual look in the mirror and decide that they no longer want to feel sick, fatigued, and unhappy with their body and health?

The guidance in the chapter on motivation holds value here as well. Edward Deci provides us with insight into the reality that each individual needs to commit to change, which is a deep personal and autonomous decision. Attempts to change a behavior at the request of others or with others in mind is usually not successful in the long run. What value do doctors' warnings and recommendations hold if the person does not want the change for themselves? There is a requirement for truthful introspection and figuring out ones "why." If this "why" is grounded in only logical and rational health-based reasons, there may not be adequate motivational energy provided by the Conscious Self for long-term success. Ideally, the motivational energies of the Basic Self are on board as well, through vivid imagery or reward strategies, to build the excitement needed for a long and possibly arduous health journey.

Once an individual connects food to health, comes to terms with the fact that what they are eating is directly negatively impacting their health, makes the autonomous decision to change, and has built up adequate motivation, several strategies can be implemented to lessen sugar/refined carb intake. Here are four options:

Crowding out – this is the main technique I learned during my health coaching studies. It involves steadily adding healthy foods that one likes, which increases the amount of quality, healthy food over time in the diet, and slowly decreases problematic foods. I usually worked with clients for six to 12 months with solid success rates. Most importantly, everyone benefited from the simple fact that they had the opportunity to discuss their health and wellness with me twice a month for a couple hours, significantly more time than they would otherwise discuss their health with anyone. This process created accountability for their behavior change as each meeting involved reviewing the prior meeting's wellness goals and ensured continuous focus on their health. Overall, health coaches can serve as valuable support systems for long-term health-related behavior change. Think about how often you discuss your health with another person who can provide guidance and insight. Most people tend not to have the opportunity outside of their yearly physical or if they go to the doctor for specific issues.

The benefits of crowding out tend to happen within a few weeks and often involve feeling better and having more energy and/or no longer crashing midday. Once this happens, the individual tends to gain more motivation to continue moving forward with the dietary adjustments. Some ways one can begin crowding out sugar is by replacing sodas and other sugary beverages with flavored water, tea, or beverages with less sugar. Moving from a can of soda which contains 40 grams of sugar to one with 10 grams (but no problematic sugar alternatives such as aspartame) is progress and a small win. Just as I, in the role of a health coach, would meet an individual where they are at in their health journey and move forward from there on a realistic and attainable path, it's important to be cognizant of where you are at this time and be truthful with yourself as to the steps you are willing to take to make positive health changes in your life. If the first step is adding some banana slices into the milk in lieu of excessive sugary cereal, so be it. This can eventually progress to a banana with almond butter, and so on.

Carbohydrate Mindfulness - this process involves the development of a thought pattern where the individual becomes cognizant of sugar and refined carbohydrates at every meal and incorporates alternatives to these foods. One of the first steps in addressing any problem is to be aware of it. Consider a standard, balanced plate of food that someone may have for dinner. It may include a meat or poultry, white rice or pasta, and a veggie. If we keep the protein and vegetable, how can we minimize or replace the carbohydrate? One option includes more vegetables and protein, to completely crowd out the rice or pasta. I did this very often during my food experiment where my dinner plate was a meat/poultry and vegetables only. Another option is transitioning the protein into a salad that also contains natural fats such as avocado and nuts, plus a complex carbohydrate such as beans. A third option is one of my all-time most successful and effectively efficient dishes, that being black beans, onions, peppers, and tomatoes, all cooked in a pot with salsa. This can fill two-thirds of a plate combined with a protein of choice and can also be topped with avocado and sour cream. When reading food labels, stay away from any foods where the carbohydrate content dominates and instead aim for a balance of macronutrients. Carbohydrate mindfulness does not necessitate the complete elimination of sugar and refined carbs, it's a state of awareness that what you are putting in your body is problematic, and alternatives are available to still enjoy your food and be full at the end of the meal.

The Habit Loop – for some, the sugar and refined carb triggers may also be connected to habits. According to the author of *The Power of Habit*, Charles Duhigg, the habit loop is a three-step process involving a cue, the routine or behavior, and a reward. In our situation, the routine is consumption of sugary foods, the reward is likely all aspects of the physical pleasure response associated with eating sugar, including the release of dopamine, but what is the cue? That may be a bit different for everyone. Do you reach for sugar when you're stressed? Is it when you're bored? Is it right after you get into a fight with your partner? Or when you feel depressed? Or right after dinner, like me? If you can figure out the cue that leads to the consumption of sugar, you can attempt other behaviors that will yield the same reward whenever you identify the cue. One solution is swapping out the sugar for a piece of fruit, which still provides a similar sweet reward that is buffered by fiber. Maybe the replacement food is dark chocolate, or something that is not food at all but still provides a sense of pleasure, such as a quick physical activity or listening to music, both of which tap into dopamine. The habit loop requires effort and introspection to figure out exactly what is triggering the consumption of sugar to begin replacing the problematic behavior.

Cold Turkey – for some, the best path may be removing sugar and simple carbs completely, all at once, which is quite a lift. One advantage to this is that if the individual can make it through approximately one month not eating sweets, tastebuds tend to adjust accordingly and if sugary treats are ever reintroduced, they may not taste as good. My personal experience with this was eliminating candy bars and other milk chocolate sweets. I distinctly remember reintroducing a snickers bar after not eating one for a couple years – it was too sweet and didn't taste as good as I remembered. The experience was a bit of a downer but eye opening at the same time and consuming milk chocolate has not been a pleasurable experience ever since. The habit loop was a part of this process as I replaced the candy bars with dark chocolate. My sweet tooth didn't go anywhere, the cue (after dinner) is always there, I just found a better alternative to address it. Over time, I worked my way up from 70% to 85-90% dark chocolate.

The cold turkey route can be greatly enhanced by not buying the sugary stuff and having it in the home. It's a lot easier to walk into the kitchen, open the freezer, and grab the ice cream then to get in the car and drive to the nearest store for the same fix. I love ice cream! But you'll rarely see it in my freezer because if it's there, I will eat it. Again, everything comes down to you and your motivation. For some, the slow and gradual elimination is the best option, for others complete elimination of everything on a certain date works great, and some individuals are somewhere in the middle of these two paths. John's story is a great example of a very specific moment that motivated him to choose one of these paths.

John's Story

In 2021, during the month of August, John took his wife and kids on a family vacation to Myrtle Beach, South Carolina. This trip was a great opportunity for him to reconnect with a very familiar environment – the ocean. Having grown up on the Jersey Shore, he had spent countless days on the beach playing, swimming, and surfing. This was his comfort zone, a second home. During one of the family's visits to the beach on a hot August day, John went into the ocean to cool down. He walked out until the water was approximately waist deep and let the small, gentle waves intermittently press against his torso. After a few minutes, he realized something was not right. John began to feel disoriented and unstable. The same ocean that he was so intimately connected to was no longer a place of comfort. What he initially perceived as forceless waves began to impact his balance. Eventually, one wave caused John to fall over and knocked a pair of $200 Oakley sunglasses off his head and into the water. Unable to quickly retrieve the glasses and no longer able to safely stand in the water, John crawled out of the ocean and into the sand. Highly upset about losing his expensive glasses and humbled by the same ocean that was his sanctuary for so many years, John realized in that moment he had to make a change.

During the week of his Myrtle Beach vacation, John weighed 360 pounds. He was diagnosed with Multiple Sclerosis (MS) ten years prior and was aware that the medication he took had a side effect of weight gain, as well as causing havoc on his joints. Over the years, he followed the guidance of his doctors in efforts to navigate MS and maintain a healthy weight, to the best of his ability. The usual recommendation which he received from the medical community for enhancement of health was to eat fruits, vegetables, and grains, cut calories, exercise, etc. Unfortunately, none of that worked for him. Over the years, John rationalized that being overweight was normal. Until that moment on the beach changed everything.

Once he and his family returned from vacation, John began to research ways to get healthy. He did this until October. During these months, he also ran into one of his wife's friends for the first time in a while, who he had remembered as being overweight. She no longer was as she had lost around 90lbs. His wife's friend shared with John that she had utilized a ketogenic diet to great success. In short, the ketogenic diet requires a significant restriction in carbohydrate intake while increasing healthy fats and protein. The combination of his research and the success story of someone he knew led to the choice of a ketogenic diet as John's path towards a healthier life. A few weeks later, John grabbed a calendar, flipped through it, and pointed at a random Sunday to serve as the beginning of his change process – his finger landing on Superbowl Sunday 2022.

In the first week of being on the ketogenic diet, John lost 13lbs, a good amount of it being water weight. This significantly boosted his motivation. He also downloaded a keto app to guide his dietary choices although he only found it useful for that purpose during the first three months. Around the three-month period, John normalized his eating and only used the app for measurement purposes moving forward. When he started his health journey, John also set a goal of eventually reaching 225lbs. As he continued to lose weight, he donated all his old clothes. He was determined not to return to his prior heavy weight and no longer owning the larger clothes motivated him further. Another motivational tool was John following Dr. Ken Berry's YouTube channel and watching all the available videos. Even though he'd never met Dr. Berry, a proponent of the ketogenic diet, John gave him a lot of credit for his success and incorporated other healthy habits, such as reading ingredient lists, through Dr. Berry's guidance.

Outside of the weight loss, John noticed other physical benefits, which included an increase in energy, confidence, and a resolution of his psoriasis symptoms. He developed the ability to connect how food made him feel, including food's impact on his mood and clarity, a skill he did not possess before. The MS no longer impacted him as it had in the past. As of April 30th, 2023, John weighed 227lbs, two pounds away from his goal weight. He no longer wears a 5x shirt, now more comfortable in an extra-large, and his waist size is down to 34 inches from a peak of 40. His latest bloodwork was pristine, and he's significantly lowered internal inflammation. He recently purchased a bicycle and plans on riding it regularly, something he has not done in over 20 years. Lastly, during John's health journey, his mom noticed the progress and began using the ketogenic diet as well – she's already lost 87lbs and was taken off several prescribed medications.

John's incredible success in bettering his health and his life is due to dietary changes alone, as at no point did he incorporate any structured exercise into his health regimen. Staying very strict to the keto dietary guidelines led to him losing over 100lbs. These guidelines required him to take the cold turkey route to reducing not only simple but all carbohydrates. Any straying from this strictness would most likely have led to lesser levels of success. Furthermore, even though the scale may not be the ideal measurement device for health success, John found value in regularly weighing himself.

As we finished up our conversation at his workplace, John wanted to share one final story with me. A few months prior, his 14-year-old daughter was getting ready for school in the morning. On her way out the door, John was feeling a bit playful and asked her for a goodbye hug, something a bit out of the norm for his teenager. In her efforts to avoid her father's embrace, his daughter took off down the street, with John close behind. Still feeling playful and in pursuit, John went into a jog. Eventually, his daughter turned around to see if her father was close, quickly processed the scene and said, "Daddy, you're running." In that moment, John realized that he had never run with his daughter before and began to cry. Instances like this continued to reinforce John's decision to take his health into his own hands and stay true to his path of success.

Listed below are a few take-home points from John's story:

- John was significantly overweight and suffering from metabolic syndrome.

- John's dietary intervention was appropriate for his health situation, that being a ketogenic diet which can be a successful strategy for weight loss and chronic disease. Hence, the intervention matched the severity of the health issues.

- John did not utilize any exercise or movement interventions during his health journey.

Is a ketogenic diet for everyone? Likely not. For some, like John, it can be an excellent tool towards better health, but others may not attain his level of benefits, or be able to adhere to it. One of the biggest issues is staying true to the diet as it is difficult to follow due to the severe restriction in carbohydrates. One's level of motivation will determine success. John built up the necessary motivation and applied the right strategy to reach his goals.

Eat Plenty of Vegetables

This section of the chapter can be summarized succinctly in seven words from nutrition journalist Michael Pollan's best seller, *In Defense of Food*. Those seven words are as follows: "Eat food. Not too much. Mostly plants." The first five words speak to eating real food in moderation, while the last two recommend that a good portion of our daily plates should possess a plethora of vegetation. This, of course, is probably not news to you, as there is consensus among nutrition experts that eating vegetables is good for us. The health benefits of vegetable consumption have been trumpeted for many years, though once we get into the weeds of this recommendation, there is a difference of opinion regarding whether some vegetables should be consumed in moderation or at all, such as white potatoes (which yield a high glycemic load that spikes blood glucose) or nightshade family vegetables (which are high in lectins that may cause inflammation in some). Yet even these controversial veggies still hold nutritional value.

Leafy greens are your no-doubt-about-it, good for you plant food (barring any specific allergies). They are an excellent place to begin building your vegetable portfolio. Even though they are an extremely important piece of the puzzle and the incorporation of leafy greens such as spinach, kale, and Bok choy alone hold great dietary value, there is a reason why you may have been advised to "eat the rainbow" at some point in your life (not to be confused with Skittles catchphrase, "Taste the Rainbow"). The greater the variety of vegetables we eat, the better. As Pollan points out in his work, different vegetables "have different antioxidants, and so help the body eliminate different kinds of toxins

(p. 163)." Considering toxin exposure is a legitimate health concern, is often unknown to the one being exposed, and sometimes unescapable, it makes sense to eat a cornucopia of vegetables to mitigate toxin exposure and for preventative purposes.

Outside of Pollan, the support for vegetable consumption is profound. Dr. Neal Barnard has written ample books on the benefits of a plant-based diet, with one of his recommendations being to eat vegetables in-season as out-of-season plant foods may not contain the level of vitamins due to excessive time in travel and storage (Barnard 1993). If one cannot attain in-season vegetables from local farmer's markets or if you live in a climate where it's not feasible to buy locally year-round, frozen vegetables are usually the next best choice. Dr. Josh Axe also supports locally grown vegetables, specifically organic to avoid genetically modified organisms (GMOs), pesticides, and herbicides. Further benefits of organic produce include a higher mineral content and higher antioxidant levels. Per guidance from Dr. Josh Axe in *Eat Dirt*: if you had the choice of rinsing your locally purchased organic carrots under running water versus scrubbing the carrots with a brush and a produce wash, go with the former because "the surface area of every carrot contains beneficial microbes" (p. 52), which benefit our gut health.

In his book, *The Microbiome Diet*, Dr. Raphael Kellman provides a list of foods which are ideal for gut health. It is no surprise that the vegetable section of this list is by far the largest, with more than 25 different vegetables listed. Some of these, such as asparagus, carrots, radishes, jicama, and tomatoes nourish healthy gut bacteria and are considered natural probiotics. In his New York Times Best Seller, *Wheat Belly*, Dr. William Davis states that "vegetables, in all their wonderous variety, are the best foods on the planet" (p. 206). To the point of variety, Dr. Davis recommends exhausting one's efforts in trying many vegetable types to find what one likes, instead of dismissing veggies due to minimal or underwhelming experience with this almighty food group. Also, vegetables should not be limited to the dinner plate only but instead be an option during all daily meals. Entrepreneur and nutritional biohacker

Dave Asprey also supports vegetables in his book, *The Bulletproof Diet*, as they should constitute more of the diet than any other food. Asprey specifies the following vegetables as nutritionally exceptional, therefore "bulletproof": asparagus, cauliflower, celery, fennel, Bok choy, broccoli, and brussels sprouts (the last three should be cooked). He also includes olives, cucumbers, and avocado which are botanically fruit. On the flip side, Asprey warns about eating canned vegetables which are usually contaminated with bisphenol A (BPA), contain preservatives, and additives to enhance shelf life. If fresh vegetables are not available and the choice is between canned and frozen, he suggests going with frozen because "frozen vegetables are far superior to canned because they are normally picked and frozen at the peak of freshness and aren't tampered with like canned vegetables" (p. 161). Frozen vegetables are a staple in my efficiently effective home-cooked meals.

Fiber

Outside of the beneficial vitamins, minerals, and antioxidants in vegetables, fiber is another major reason to consume plant foods. Aside from vegetables, other high fiber foods include nuts, seeds, legumes, and fruit. The Standard American Diet lacks greatly in the fiber department. In their 2020 research, "The Health Benefits of Dietary Fiber", Barber et al. discussed the negative health implications of a diet low in fiber, as well as the positive health outcomes associated with the optimization of fiber in the diet. The dietary fiber benefits they mention include a healthy gut microbiome, reduced risk of cardiovascular disease, reduced inflammation, increased insulin sensitivity, and favorable body weight. The researchers also made an important point in their conclusion regarding our current dietary habits: "The problem is that what most of us consider normal is actually highly abnormal and about as far away from what our hominid hunter-gatherer ancestors experienced and enjoyed as it is possible to imagine" (p. 11). When the totality of human history on planet earth is taken into consideration, the Standard American Diet is the epitome of an anomaly. It's the ultimate outlier.

It's someone mistaking a shopping mall for a nude beach and arriving at the entrance in their birthday suit. The reality that we live in a food environment that requires self-education, at least middle-class wealth, strategic food shopping, discipline, and motivation to enhance our chances of extending health span is a testament to the unusuality of current times.

Fat and Protein

Consensus regarding how much fat and protein we should consume daily is lacking. The latest USDA Dietary Guidelines provide wide ranges of 20 to 35 percent for daily fat intake, and 10 to 35 percent for daily protein intake. It's fair to assume that if a person consumed 35 percent fat, 35 percent protein, and the remaining 30 percent carbohydrate daily, their health outcomes may differ from someone who consumed 20 percent fat, 10 percent protein, and 70 percent carbohydrate – even if both happen to eat high quality food. The Guidelines further recommend consuming less than 10 percent of calories per day from saturated fats, the exact same percentage as sugar. Without going too deep into the matter, all saturated fat is not the same. For example, "the type of saturated fat found in coconut oil, a plant source, is different from the type found in animal products" (Fife 1999, p. 5). The medium chain triglycerides found in coconut oil have been shown to play a role in decreasing abdominal obesity, inflammation, and metabolic syndrome, and enhancing exercise performance (Wang 2018). It is questionable that the recommended restrictions for saturated fat and sugar are the same considering that books have been written on the health benefits of coconut oil, butter, and ghee – all forms of saturated fat and all three food staples in different cultures for centuries. I'm not aware of any literature touting the health benefits of sugar. Outside of these saturated fat examples, there are other quality sources of dietary fat worth incorporating into the diet, such as avocado, nuts, seeds, olive oil, and eggs.

Recommendations for daily protein intake is a debated topic. The current recommended daily allowance (RDA) in the United States for a healthy adult with minimal physical activity is 0.8 grams per kilogram (kg) of body weight per day. For someone who weighs 150 pounds, that's around 54 grams of protein per day. The recommendation goes up incrementally based on physical activity and doubles to 1.6 grams per kg of body weight for individuals who perform intense physical activity. Going up to two grams per kg of body weight is safe for healthy adults (Wu 2016). In a recent paper, Weiler et al. (2023) recommended a re-evaluation of the current RDA and concluded that "Historical data and new evidence on health and functional outcomes for adults and the pregnant population generally support higher protein recommendations" (p. 23). Further support for higher protein intake comes from research on high protein diets and weight loss. Per Moon and Koh (2020):

> Several clinical trials have found that consuming more protein than the recommended dietary allowance not only reduces body weight (BW), but also enhances body composition by decreasing fat mass while preserving fat-free mass (FFM) in both low-calorie and standard-calorie diets. Fairly long-term clinical trials of 6–12 months reported that a high-protein diet (HPD) provides weight-loss effects and can prevent weight regain after weight loss (p. 166).

High protein diets were beneficial for weight loss because they increased satiety and energy expenditure. Interestingly, the percentage of protein consumed daily in some of these studies (27 to 35 percent) was around the percentage I consumed during my self-experiment discussed in the appendix. As with the other macronutrients, the quality of the protein matters. If financially feasible for the consumer, the sources of meat, poultry, and fish deemed the highest quality are grass-fed, pasture-raised, and wild caught. For vegetarian sources, tofu and edamame (non-GMO ideally), lentils, beans, chia seeds, and nut butters are quality options.

Effectively Efficient Cooking

So how do we get a wide variety of vegetables in our bodies in the shortest time possible each day? First, consider that cooking is non-negotiable – one must cook and/or prep most meals and not outsource them to the outside world, losing control of the ingredients in the process. When we take control of our food, we begin to take control of our health. But this is not only about eating healthy; the goal is to eat healthy AND be effectively efficient as well. If you are busy and you don't have an hour every day for meal prep and cooking, this section is for you! There are four specific ways in which I've managed to enhance my vegetable consumption and created healthy meals while spending no more than 15-20 minutes with meal prep and cooking, and sometimes cleaning time, combined. Let's begin with the stir fry.

Stir Fry

This starts with the ownership of a large enough frying or stir fry pan into which you can throw copious amounts of vegetables, among other healthful goodies. I'm a huge fan of organic frozen veggies and there are bags of them in my freezer year-round. I live in New Jersey hence during the winter months fresh, locally grown produce is not an option. As mentioned before, these vegetables are frozen at their peak, hence the nutritional value quality should not be compromised. My preferred option is the 365 Wholefoods organic brand and I like to purchase the mixes and medleys to ensure that I am getting an assortment of vegetables in my body daily. I usually cook my stir fry on coconut or ghee. I'm not overly concerned about the amount of fat but about the quality. I try to stay away from cooking fats like vegetable and canola oil, which are high in omega-6 fatty acids and may add to the already problematic omega-6 to omega-3 ratios in the American diet. Ideally, this ratio is three-to-one, yet for most Americans it greatly sways in the direction of omega-6s, which may trigger inflammation.

As the frozen vegetables soften up in the pan, I add whatever fresh vegetables are in my fridge, along with a source of protein, nuts or seeds, and finally some coconut aminos, teriyaki sauce, tamari, or sesame oil for flavor. This entire cooking process should take no more than 15 minutes and requires minimal work – just put things in a pan, lift the lid occasionally and stir. I don't add any rice nor noodles to my stir fry, but a whole grain may be an option.

The Omelet

The almighty omelet, what a great opportunity for creative dietary efficiency. I'm sure at some point in your life you've seen a veggie omelet on a diner's menu. Maybe you've tried it. Usually these consist of eggs, broccoli, peppers, onions, maybe spinach. These vegetables are a great start but the options of healthful items that can go into an omelet are limitless. The omelet making process starts the same as the stir fry process, although I do not cook omelets on coconut oil, sticking mostly to ghee or butter. Just be mindful that ghee has a significantly higher smoking point than butter, hence if you're going to cook on butter, don't use high heat.

As with the stir fry, frozen veggies are an option here although I like to focus on fresh vegetables for omelets. Mushrooms are a fantastic addition too, or you can go with the mushroom's flavor of umami seasoning. Add salt, pepper, and/or paprika as well. The next step is dependent on whether you want the omelet to be a protein-rich meal and hit 25-30 grams of protein per meal, especially as the first meal of the day. If so, I would suggest ½ cup of black beans and three eggs, which combined with whatever vegetables you already used, should put the meal into the 25-30 grams of protein range. An alternative to the beans is sunflower seeds, specifically ¼ cup, and the three eggs.

Once the omelet is cooked, the addition of a half of an avocado on top as another healthy source of fat is a great move. If you went with the black bean protein option, add some salsa and something spicy, if that's your thing. Again, prep and cooking time, no more than 10-15 minutes, if not less. We are doing nothing more here than throwing healthy things into a pan. Also, most veggies are a go when it comes to omelets, but you may want to skip the potatoes as they have a high glycemic load.

Shakes/Smoothies

Before I get into the specifics of shakes and smoothies (I'm going to use the word "shakes" for the rest of this section), ownership of a quality blender holds significant value. If there is one kitchen appliance that I would suggest splurging on, it's the blender. Aside from personal experience with cheap blenders that created chalky concoctions or led to chewing on small pieces of unblended kale, I've heard plenty of people complain about not being able to make a tasty, quality shake. It starts with the blender. I've owned the Vitamix brand for 12 years now and have zero complaints about my shakes unless I create something gross myself. This is a worthy investment, whether you go with a Vitamix or another quality brand.

I've been making shakes for over 20 years and have never used a recipe. The important thing to know here is that vegetables must be in the blender along with whatever fruits you choose to incorporate. Most tend to enjoy a tasty, fruit-only shake from a local smoothie shop, which is often purported as a healthy choice even though aside from the fruit, there is the probability of added sweeteners. Yes, you may get some nutritional value from a fruit-only shake, but the sugar content is not ideal (unless it's berries only). My two favorite leafy greens for shakes which tend not to overwhelm the flavor, are spinach and kale. A handful of each is a great nutritional enhancement. I've used plenty of other veggies in shakes over the years, such as jicama, beets, carrots, cucumbers, broccoli, romaine lettuce, mint, and ginger. There is a place for avocado in all my shakes as it's not only a healthy fat, but it also makes the shake smooth and thick, which I prefer over a runny concoction. Occasionally, due to my love for ice cream, I'll make the shake so thick using avocado and ice that it mimics an ice cream eating experience. This serves as a healthy alternative to ice cream in my habit loop. Furthermore, you can incorporate nuts in your shake for more healthy fats and some protein. If you want to turn this into a complete meal, you can add a protein powder just do some research first to ensure that you are using a reputable protein brand. The protein shake I used in the self-experiment outlined in the appendix was very simple and included the following along with grass-fed whey: banana, walnuts, avocado, almond or coconut milk, sometimes strawberries, and ice.

Prior to incorporating daily intermittent fasting which includes skipping breakfast, I used to substitute the almond or coconut milk with coffee and drink my shake in the morning. Coffee shakes are now available at many places, although again, be careful regarding added sugars if you are going to take this route. Nowadays I consume my shake as either my first meal of the day during lunchtime, or around 5:00 to 6:00pm.

Salads

This is a no-brainer, so we are not going to spend much time here. Your salad should be predominantly vegetables. My only suggestion is to make the salad a complete meal as sometimes folks go on a salad craze and walk around hungry all day. Add plenty of fat and protein to the salad, such as beans, chicken, avocado, olives, and a quality dressing of your choice, taking sugar content into consideration.

One important concept to understand when it comes to eating vegetables is bioavailability – the amount of a nutrient from the food you eat that is absorbed and used by the body. This concept reframes the age-old quote, "You are what you eat" to the more accurate, "You are what you digest." Just because a cup of spinach has six percent of your daily magnesium does not mean your body is able to attain and utilize all that magnesium. Our digestive systems vary greatly based on many factors, and we really do not know how much of a nutrient our body is able to absorb and use, hence overfocusing on percentages on food labels may not be the ideal move. This brings us back to focusing on the food itself and ensuring that we are getting a plethora of different veggies to enhance the nutritional potential in our daily meals. There is also the option of a daily multivitamin as well as other supplements such as vitamin D3, omega-3 fatty acids, and magnesium, to name a few of the most important ones. Vitamins and their value in the human diet have been a subject of significant contention for many years. In cases when an individual's diet is grossly lacking in nutrients or they have a deficiency, vitamins may be of benefit.

Chapter 8

Fasting

An integral part of cultural and religious norms for many centuries, fasting has become a common strategy in the realm of health and wellness, often utilized for weight loss. There is a variety of different ways one can incorporate this strategy, from not eating for a specific amount of time each day, to limiting calories on certain days during the week, to not eating for a whole day, two days, three days, and so on. Considering fasting takes zero time to incorporate, it wreaks of effective efficiency. Before delving into the specifics of this practice and whether it yields legitimate health benefits, it's worth seeing how the combination of fasting and other health strategies changed one man's life.

Joey's Story

In the latter months of 2020, Joey had reached his highest weight ever, fluctuating in the 300–315-pound range. He was stressed out and overwhelmed while doing his best to be a father, husband, and support system for not only his immediate family but others as well. These dynamics were compounded by the coronavirus pandemic and the day-to-day uncertainty, fear, and anxiety that he and millions of others experienced. Joey lived in a State that maintained very strict COVID protocols, which was another difficult adjustment for him as he was usually a social person. Navigating this new way of life combined with a lack of established self-care tools took a significant toll on Joey's body and mind.

One Friday night, Joey lay in the fetal position, the body's instinctual response to extreme stress and trauma. The overwhelm was no longer manageable and Joey's mind had reached its breaking point. As he lay there, feeling completely helpless, his wife asked him a very simple question: "Who are you?" because she did not know this version of her husband. As time passed and he continued to lay in a state of primal self-preservation, Joey pondered her inquiry and eventually concluded that he had choice. No matter how much life threw at him, ultimately the response to the stimuli was his choice. Within 48 hours, the first choice he made in response to his current situation was to incorporate some form of self-care.

The next day, Joey game planned how he would incorporate intermittent fasting into his life. That Sunday night, he stopped eating at 8:00pm and did not eat again until 12pm on Monday, totaling 16 hours of fasting. Joey drank calorie-free black coffee in the mornings instead of eating breakfast. Over the next weeks and months, he started incorporating simple physical activity into his life – walking around the block in his neighborhood. During that time, he also began a progressive process of decreasing sugar intake, which started with cutting out soda and beer.

In the early stages of change, Joey experience discomfort and withdrawal as his body was adjusting to this new way of life. He also had to deal with the hunger pangs of fasting but eventually his body adjusted to that as well. His perseverance was essential to the continued progression and positive shifts which he soon experienced. For the first time in a long time, Joey felt a sense of sustained clarity. This led to better decision making and enhancement of his organizational abilities. Next, came the increase in energy which led to feeling better and being more productive every day. These initial health benefits boosted Joey's motivation to continue with intermittent fasting and the dietary changes he already incorporated, plus experiment with some more.

The next steps in Joey's health progression involved substituting healthy snacks for less healthy ones, restricting more simple and refined carbohydrates, and incorporating more healthy foods. For example, he substituted nuts for potato chips as a snack, became mindful of bread and pasta consumption, and began eating salads as meals. Prior to the initial positive health changes, Joey would have never considered a salad as a meal. Yet, already experiencing numerous benefits opened his mind towards further dietary experimentation. Over time, in efforts to enhance his physical activity, he also incorporated resistance bands for at-home workouts.

During his health journey, Joey lost a lot of weight without counting or reducing calories, nor any excessive exercise/physical exertion. In fact, Joey was adamant that the gym would not have been a benefit to his progress due to it being an intimidating environment. To the contrary, if he went that route, it may have derailed his progress. For many, the gym can be the key to unlocking long-term fitness and health, but that does not mean it's an across-the-board recommendation for all who want to enhance health and feel better.

In April 2023, Joey sat in front of me at a local Starbucks still clear-minded, still energetic, and 185 pounds. He's continued intermittent fasting daily with black coffee, likes nuts and salads, and no longer drank soda. The benefits he experienced in his life go way beyond the mental and physical. With his newfound energy and clarity came work-related production which opened professional doors that were not open before. As a natural risk taker, Joey took some calculated risks, transitioned workplaces, and is currently positioned to become very successful in his field of work. I asked him if the professional growth would have been possible if he was still the late 2020 version of himself. As you'd probably expect, the answer was no. I also asked Joey if he can ever see himself going back to his old ways that did not involve much if any self-care. His answer – "absolutely not." Outside of all these positives, life continued to throw Joey occasional curveballs, but in his current form, he is physically and mentally equipped to better deal with stress and uncertainty.

Joey's journey led to the belief that personal growth and progression starts with a change in mentality. One of his most painful and vulnerable moments led to the empowered understanding that he had choice. This epiphany led to motivation to incorporate healthy change. There was the expected initial physical and mental discomfort, but he persevered past that, began to see benefits from his new behaviors, which enhanced motivation to continue what he was doing and add more positive change. Further success skyrocketed motivation and life presented opportunities that he would not have been cognizant of in his prior physical and mental state. What was initially healthy behavior change is now ingrained as a long-term lifestyle. A crucial part of this process was Joey picking health-related behavior changes that worked for him, specifically intermittent fasting and reduction in simple and refined carbohydrates. I reached out to Joey towards the end of summer in 2024, to see how he was doing. He's down another ten pounds of weight and enjoying time with his daughters thrift shopping and playing wiffleball in the backyard.

Personal Experience with Fasting

Joey's success is an example of combining "what" to eat, or more importantly, what not to eat, which are principles we've already discussed, and introduces our next topic, the "when" to eat, and more specifically, fasting. I incorporated fasting into my life in 2018. The reason for it: I probably read something about fasting and thought trying it might benefit my health. My first fast involved a 16-hour fasting window from a Sunday evening into the next Monday morning, during which time I skipped breakfast. Eventually, I became intrigued with how long I could fast for and extended to 18 hours, and very quickly after that, 24 hours. But why stop at a day of no food? I soon pushed to 36 hours and then a full two days with zero calories. Fasting was the first time I began to incorporate coffee into my daily routine because it significantly curbed my appetite – and by coffee, I mean black coffee only. To this day, coffee is a fasting vehicle for me versus a cream and sugar filled beverage of enjoyment. Although the bitterness brings a bit of pleasure.

One of the best things that happened during this fasting phase of my life was motivating a few friends and my wife to fast with me. There was a core group of us, around five to six, who would push each other through the 48-hour fasts. This epitomized the benefits of having a support group when one moves forth with any health initiatives. Returning to the work of Duhigg and habits, being a member of a group when attempting any behavior change can enhance success and build belief. During this time, I conducted some deeper reading into fasting, specifically another book by Dr. Fung, *The Complete Guide to Fasting*, and became intrigued with prolonged fasting. How long could I go without food? One thing I learned during the 48-hour fasts, and it's something that most seasoned fasters will tell you, is that one does not feel hungry while fasting. It seems counterintuitive, but it's true, at least it was for me. With the assistance of black coffee, tea, and water, and without being overwhelmed by food cues such as being around food all day or smelling it constantly, I was very much ok with zero food in my life – for at most two days. If I could go 48 hours without food, why not try five full days? Yes, 120 hours. I talked my wife Ganga and two friends, Julian and Detrik, into doing this with me. We decided to stop eating on a Sunday night at 7:00pm and not eat again until the next Friday 7:00pm.

My wife was the first to reintroduce food 48 hours in – an impressive fast, nonetheless. The next one to eat was Julian, around the 60-hour mark. Mid-Wednesday, Detrik and I remained, and we supported each other all the way to Friday evening. You may be wondering what the experience was like, how we felt throughout, and the results. It was the equivalent of a roller coaster ride with one drop and a loop.

The mental and physical familiarity with completing prior 48-hour fasts was helpful and led to a smooth first two days. Interestingly, day two seems to be when fasters have difficulties with hunger (Fung 2016). The beginning of day three absolutely sucked. I sat at my desk miserable, rethinking the fasting journey. Up to that point, black coffee was my best friend but on day three it turned heel on me and became gross. For the rest of the fast, I only drank water and tea. On day four, I rebounded strong. That morning, I drove halfway across the state of New Jersey and taught a basic self-defense class. Upon my return home, I took on solo parent duties while my wife went out with friends.

Day five was a mixed bag. It started off well but once it got closer to 7:00pm, I began feeling antsy and generally not well, likely because my mind was hyper fixated on eating again. Around 5:00pm, the thought of how I was going to break the fast crossed my mind for the first time. While at the local shopping mall with my family, I pulled out my phone and read a couple articles about how to properly break an extended fast. Apparently, eating a couple slices of pizza was not the ideal way to do it. The suggested method was to consume a small snack first, chew thoroughly, drink water throughout the process, take it slow, and consume the main meal 30 to 60 minutes after the snack (Fung 2016).

After attaining this insight and with less than two hours to go before we broke the fast, I texted Detrik and advised him to break it gently. As I feared, his initial food choice was far from gentle – a Wendy's chicken sandwich. Thankfully, he took my advice and drove to his local supermarket to purchase bone broth, cauliflower, and other ingredients for a soup (which he claimed was the best thing he ever tasted). I broke my fast with a small bowl of soft, cooked root vegetables and a touch of kimchi. Over the next few days, I mostly consumed probiotic foods such as kraut and kimchi, cooked vegetables, as well as bone broth and supplemented with L-glutamine. After the initial post-fast days, I re-introduced raw vegetables and some fish protein.

That first bite of food after not eating for five days was a powerful experience. A couple bites in, I was flooded with emotions and shed a few tears. It's hard to explain why this happened, but in that moment, I appreciated food like I've never appreciated it before. Not eating for that long put the value of eating into perspective and made the experience euphoric. One of my goals during the extended fast was to see if I could tap into something deeper, something spiritual. Unfortunately, that evaded me during the fast. The day-to-day hustle, working and parenting two kids, provided little opportunity for reflection and appreciation of this experience. At that point in my life, I had yet to tap into a deeper sense of self. But that first bite of food was extremely powerful and worth the five-day journey.

I lost some weight during the extended fast. I started the fast at 156 pounds and ended it at 145.2 pounds. My body fat decreased from 8.35% to 7.55%. My friend lost 15.4 pounds (he started off at a heavier weight than me, hence the weight loss was proportional to mine). Other benefits included clearing up of rosacea and increased mental clarity for Detrik and lowering of blood pressure for me. There is research that supports our changes. Wilhelmi de Toledo et al. (2019) conducted an observational study of 1422 subjects who fasted between 4 to 21 days. The findings included significant reductions in weight, waist circumference, and blood pressure, along with increased physical and emotional well-being. In line with my extended fasting experience, 93.2 percent of subjects reported absence of hunger. If you are considering an extended fast, please consult with your doctor if you have any chronic health concerns.

Benefits of Fasting

Fasting is the most effectively efficient diet-related behavioral change because it takes zero minutes out of your day. If implemented into an existing schedule, it's very convenient. There is no food prep, no time spent cooking, creation of meal plans, and no extra money spent as you'll likely save money on a meal or two each day. The only decisions you'll need to make is the length of the fast, when you'll start and finish, and what non-caloric beverage(s) you'll consume during the fast. If fasting is for you, be mindful to work it around your daily schedule, not change your life around the fast. This will enhance the likelihood of fasting becoming a long-term behavior.

There are two lenses we can observe the health benefits of intermittent fasting through. The first is calorie restriction or simply, eating less. If minimizing the daily eating window leads to less calories consumed, this provides the same benefits as calorie restriction diets, such as weight loss, decreased waist circumference, and decreased insulin resistance – without the body eventually adjusting by slowing down metabolism. As mentioned already, long-term adherence to calorie restriction is difficult hence fasting may be a better alternative for long-term weight loss. One of the practical concerns with restricting calories is counting or being cognizant of them. With intermittent fasting, one does not have to count calories. Furthermore, "with caloric restriction, approximately one-third to one-fourth of the weight loss is known to be of lean tissue" (Anton et al. 2018, p. 11). In an eight-week study conducted on men using the 16/8 intermittent fasting window combined with resistance training (exactly what I do every day), there was a decrease in fat mass and maintenance of muscle mass (Moro et al. 2016). Bottom line: eating less daily will likely lead to indiscriminate weight loss over time while intermittent fasting may target body fat loss specifically, especially if one also weightlifts.

The second lens involves the metabolic mechanism behind the above study's results. After at least 12 hours of fasting, although this may vary, the body switches from utilizing glucose for fuel to ketone bodies (Mishra et al. 2023). Fatty acids are mobilized, and the body begins to burn stored fat. This is likely what dieters prefer, the loss of body fat specifically. Further beneficial changes include reduced inflammation, enhanced autophagy, decreased blood pressure, decreased resting heart rate, and enhanced cognition (Mattson et al. 2017). There is an evolutionary perspective on these physiological enhancements – for most of our time on earth, food was scarce and to survive the human body needed to function optimally during times of starvation.

I fast every day for 14 to 16 hours and skip breakfast in the process. I sip on black coffee throughout the morning as it suppresses my appetite. Between 12:00pm and 1:00pm, I eat my first meal and usually fit at least one more full meal and smaller meals, or two full meals before I stop eating. My last meal is two hours prior to bedtime, on average. Breakfast is the meal that is easiest for most to skip, although some prefer to skip dinner. A 2013 study found that eating a high-caloric breakfast with a reduced dinner may be useful to manage obesity and metabolic syndrome (Jukabowicz et al. 2013), hence an intermittent fast with a 7am to 3pm eating window may be ideal for those aiming to lose weight.

I find great value in skipping breakfast because not making and eating it provides me more time in the morning for other self-care techniques, specifically meditation and exercise. On the days when I wake up at 5:45am, by 7:00am, which is the time I wake my children for school, I've already meditated and exercised, as well as showered and used the bathroom. I'm ready to take on the world! This is the epitome of effective efficiency with self-care – enjoying the benefits of fasting, meditation, and exercise all day while spending minimal time on these activities in the morning.

While there is ample evidence that eating less sugar and processed foods, along with more vegetables, is beneficial to everyone, there is still more research needed to place fasting among those recommendations. I share my story and supportive research to display this strategy as worthy of consideration for health enhancement. Nevertheless, it may not be for everyone. If you've attempted some form of fasting and you've experienced benefits, as I have, it makes sense to continue with this strategy. If it was a difficult or an unpleasant experience, there are many other dietary approaches that may hold more value.

Effectively Efficient with Nutrition

Let's summarize the main points of effective efficiency in the nutrition domain:

- Significantly reduce consumption of sugar and simple/refined carbohydrates through crowding out, carbohydrate mindfulness, the habit loop, and/or going cold turkey.

- Significantly reduce consumption of processed foods.

- Four easy and quick meals that provide the opportunity to incorporate more vegetables into the diet are stir fry's, omelets, shakes, and salads – as well as anything else that you create on your own.

- Incorporating intermittent fasting may be beneficial for some, and those benefits start at 12 hours of fasting. For most, 12 hours without food each day is a worthy pursuit.

Kenya's Story

In 2016, Kenya was in graduate school, working two jobs, and raising two young children. She was constantly tired and very uncomfortable with herself as she had reached her heaviest weight of 296 pounds. For most of her adult life, Kenya considered herself heavy and a yo-yo dieter, incorporating different diets into her lifestyle that led to losing weight, gaining it back, losing it again, and eventually gaining it back. She tried Nutra system, Weight Watchers, Atkins, the grapefruit diet, you name it. Her process involved attaining some initial results, not staying dedicated, and reverting to old habits and ways of eating. Eventually, she realized that dieting just did not work for her and was not willing to go through this process anymore. One day, while spending time with her mom and stepdad, they brought up the topic of weight loss surgery. Kenya gave this option plenty of thought and eventually decided to go through with the procedure in November of 2017, specifically the gastric sleeve. She didn't make the decision with the expectation that surgery would magically solve everything, but instead went into the process knowing that she would also need to change her eating and relationship with food long term. Initially, she stuck to the dietary changes but as with her prior diet attempts, she eventually began to revert to old ways of eating.

When we discussed her past dietary habits, Kenya mentioned to me that she had never been an overeater and in 2018 concluded that she was actually undereating and slowing down her metabolism in the process. When this happens over an extended amount of time, it can lead to unpleasant feelings of fatigue and constant hunger. To help her re-establish proper eating portions, Kenya downloaded apps that focused on meal scheduling and healthy eating. Initially, it was difficult for her to eat more than she had been, but she did her best to do so. Yet even the development of this insight and new portion sizes were not enough to lead to sustainable weight loss and after completing graduate school in 2019, Kenya noticed that she was putting weight on again. Even though she had made so many attempts at reaching a healthy weight, including weight loss surgery, sustained success seemed very far away as she still hovered in the 200lb range. She was also fully cognizant of the fact that after two years following bariatric surgery, weight loss may stop, and weight gain may occur. This was exactly what began to happen.

As Kenya contemplated her continued health struggles and post-surgery weight gain, a good friend asked her to participate in the 21-day challenge through a global nutrition company. She knew that this friend had benefited through the same protocol. Although skeptical, Kenya agreed, went through, and completed the challenge, losing 12 pounds in the process. Soon after, she purchased some of the company's products, which included shakes, teas, and supplements. Kenya explained to me that this company provided her with three very important dynamics which led to eventual success: 1) a supportive and positive community, 2) flavorful and tasty products, and 3) a specific structure to eating. This combination became the catapult for Kenya to support her weight loss and health.

As she became more involved with the company, Kenya attended her first live event – she had never seen so many happy people before in one place who exuded tons of positive energy. Meeting these people and a deeper involvement in the community led to an understanding for Kenya that outside of eating right and eventually exercising, health progress can also be guided by an overall process of self-growth and personal development. This insight unlocked a deeper motivation for her. Hence, the weight loss and health gain led to an understanding of the importance of personal development, which now reinforces the healthy lifestyle – a beautiful cyclical process. This was further enhanced by Kenya seeing others succeed through physical exercise, which led to her joining fit camps and hiring a personal trainer.

As Kenya recounted her journey to me on May 11th, 2023, she was at 189lbs. Her goal was always to be under 200lbs, which she reached. She also had the understanding that since incorporating exercise and specifically resistance training, her body went through positive changes that could no longer be gauged by a scale, that being the development of muscle and changes in overall physical composition. Kenya also developed great insight into self – she advised me that she still possesses an inner fat girl mentality but is fully aware of this. She's connected her past problematic ways of eating directly to learned behavior from her parents, as her mom always worked a lot and ate on the run. I asked Kenya if there were any other benefits that she's experienced outside of the ones already mentioned. She advised that she feels the best she ever has in her adult life, has more energy, enhanced cardiovascular health, looks better, can do things physically now that she couldn't before, and has learned how to deal with negative energy in her life as well as addressing relationships that may be problematic. Recently, she visited a plus size store that has been her go-to for clothes for years. During this specific visit she was advised by the sales rep that they had nothing there for her, and she had to instead go to a local Victoria Secrets.

Outside of the benefits she's experienced, I asked Kenya what motivators keep her on track. Overall, Kenya was finally able to connect the importance of health for life. She's motivated by not wanting to be a burden to others, avoiding disease, and continues to gain inspiration from her health community. She's also realized that even though exercise holds great value, for her path and purposes, what she ate was more important. Kenya's health journey started with the gastric sleeve surgery that got her down to a comfortable weight, but it was the supportive community, tasty products, and structured eating that led to the maintenance of weight loss and a long-term lifestyle change to support her health.

There is one more very important aspect to Kenya's journey. She was able to tap into a deeper motivation that has always been a driver for her life choices, specifically regarding professional and career paths. Kenya has always felt the need to help and support others in some capacity. We initially met years ago when she began working at a shelter for runaway and abused youth where I had been working for years. Her health journey eventually tapped into this deeper driver to help others as she became a coach and ambassador of her health community. In her own words, she now wants to "help people feel the best that they can." Armed with this motivation, Kenya began taking on clients and eventually guided another person through the loss of 100lbs. This is the end game for anyone who has attained a level of success, took their process and knowledge, and focused energy to assist others in gaining success as well. Kenya's health journey eventually turned into passion, which I could gauge as she talked about her growth and all she's learned. Once she decided to shift her energy and efforts to help others, she turned her passion into purpose.

Chapter 9

Goal Setting

That First Goal

For the past nine years, on January 1st, I find a quiet space to contemplate and write down goals for that particular year. Some call this "New Year's Resolutions", I prefer goal setting. This process was not initially spurred by insight into the power of goal setting, which came much later, but instead by a feeling of professional stagnation and an urge to help others. My first goal contemplation session in 2016 yielded exactly one result: present on the topic of nutrition in front of a group of people. At that point in my life, nutrition was a side passion and I felt confident in my knowledge on this subject. I also had a few years of health coaching under my belt and decent public speaking skills. There was no clear path to completing this goal as my full-time job did not provide opportunities to present on the topic of nutrition, but I felt that if I at least wrote the goal down and put it out into the universe, something may come out of it. It wasn't much, but this one written goal was still a step above anything I'd ever done before within the realm of intentions. Interestingly, within a few months, the universe responded.

In March of that year, as I perused my organization's employee training catalog, I noticed a workshop on the topic of facilitation. I thought, "why not, I'm already somewhat good at public speaking, it's something I enjoy, why not get better at it." So, I signed up. On the first day of this three-day session, I found myself in a room with approximately 15 co-workers from different divisions of the organization, but most importantly, members of the human resources department, which included the person in charge of training. A couple hours into the training, I connected the dots – I set a goal for presenting on the topic of nutrition in front of a group of people and a few months later I am in a training about facilitation with the training coordinator of my organization also there. Later in the day I learned that on the third day of the training, each person would present on a topic of their choice in front of the class. This was my opportunity! If I could shine in front of this group and the training coordinator specifically, then I could propose to her my nutrition presentation that I set as a goal for that year.

On the third day of this training (scheduled a week after the first two days), I would technically achieve my goal because I'd present on whatever topic I wanted (of course I chose nutrition) in front of the class, but this quick 15-minute presentation was not what I had in mind when I set the goal. I wanted more time and a bigger audience, something more official. I didn't just want to be a training participant practicing facilitation in a learning setting, I wanted to be THE trainer. Yet this mini presentation was still important because it was a vehicle to display my knowledge and skill set in front of the training coordinator.

Even though all the pieces were falling in place, fear and apprehension made their obligatory appearance. I set a goal and now there was a clear path to accomplish it, but the possibility of success scared me. I considered hijacking my efforts and not taking advantage of this opportunity. The easy path would have been to stay in my comfort zone and play small. I instead rationalized that everything was playing out exactly as intended because I wrote down the goal and I would have been a fool not to follow through on the clear path that was laid before me. Over the next week, I worked hard to develop the best fifteen minutes of nutrition entertainment ever created and practiced it until I felt comfortable with the content.

On day three of the training, my hard work paid off as I nailed the presentation. I tend to assess my public speaking performances soon after I finish, and this one I deemed an instant classic. The evaluations from my co-workers in the training confirmed my self-assessment. Most importantly, the training coordinator was impressed. This was good! Yet just because I delivered in the training did not mean that she was obligated to afford me the opportunity to deliver a training on nutrition on a bigger stage. I wasn't even a formal trainer! Knowing this, just as the training was wrapping up and everyone was packing their belongings, I walked up to the training coordinator and told her that I would love to do something like what I just presented, formally as a training for the organization. She agreed that it could be something interesting. I successfully planted the seed.

I made zero effort to follow up on this seed for a few weeks because my old friend fear returned, this time in the form of fear of rejection. After mauling over the possibility of being told "no" way longer than I should have, I finally gathered the courage to reach out to someone I knew personally in the training coordinator's department. My connect set up a meeting and the next step in the process was in motion – the opportunity to sell myself and my idea for the training.

Before we move on, I should point out that I put all my eggs in one basket and did not develop alternative paths to reaching my goal. Considering it had a one-year expiration date and it was already May when the meeting with the training coordinator was set, I should have developed other options for success. Thankfully, things worked out for me.

During the meeting, I didn't have to oversell myself. I don't recall much of the conversation other than the fact that the training coordinator was very friendly, open-minded, and willing to provide me with the opportunity to present on nutrition if her superiors were on board as well. Luckily, they were and on July 13th, 2016, from 10:00am to 12:00pm, I presented a nutrition workshop titled, "Healthy Habits:

How They Can Help You on the Job" to a group of twenty-five co-workers. Goal accomplished.

Things didn't stop there because the first Health Habits workshop was a success. On August 10th, 2016, I presented another nutrition workshop with more content and built-in interaction, which was a success as well. The next year, I delivered both workshops again. Through this process I gained experience in training content development, public speaking (which I teach now), and most importantly spoke about a topic which I was very passionate about, hopefully positively impacting members of the audience in the process. All of this started with a goal that I typed into my phone. Setting that one goal opened doors and opportunities in my career that may have not otherwise materialized.

Goal Setting 101

I cannot overstate the importance and impact of goal setting. Even though my story is far from a structured and full-proof process for goal setting and accomplishment, it was a starting point for developing an appreciation for clearly defined goals – a starting point which led to the continued implementation of goal setting at the beginning of every year since. These goals, although not always realized by the end of each year, usually lead to something positive occurring in my life and personal development. They are big goals with no clear path to success that push me outside of my comfort zone.

As I mentioned before, the reason I set the initial goal was stagnation in my position at the workplace, lack of challenges, and boredom with my job duties. Boredom in the workplace tends to lead to disengagement and I did not want to be that employee who is retired at his desk, just going through the motions daily. I needed a change, and the nutrition training experience became integral in bolstering my resume and enhancing a skill set that led to me applying for a completely different position within my organization. That position was a training coordinator and on my second try, I got the job! Now I do something that I enjoy, something that provides the opportunity for creativity, and something that has catapulted me into other opportunities that would not have been possible before. Again, all of it spurred with that one goal.

The set-a-big-goal without a clear path, connect-the-dots, universe-guided method, although a fascinating path, may not always work. A more sure-fire process is to regularly develop mini goals that will ultimately lead to achieving the bigger goal. In his book, *The Art of the Impossible, a Peak Performance Primer*, Steven Kotler masterfully lays out the goal setting process. Before setting a big goal, or as Kotler termed, high, hard goal (HHG), and the smaller goals to reach it, it's beneficial to have a deeper level motivator for the big goal, an intrinsic driver. (I will use the term "big goal" instead of high, hard goal). My big goal of presenting on the topic of nutrition before a group of people was driven by the deeper need to share my nutrition knowledge with others so that I could impact their lives positively, which was my intrinsic driver, a purpose for my intended actions. Purpose involves positively impacting others and enacting change on a larger scale. Following formal learning, I enhanced my nutritional knowledge through self-learning because I had passion for this subject matter. Any goals supported by passion and purpose have a higher likelihood of accomplishment. To clarify further:

- My Purpose – Impact people positively by teaching them about healthy eating.

- My Passion – Continuously attain knowledge in the field of nutrition.

- My Big Goal – Present on the topic of nutrition in front of a group of people.

- My Mini Goals – The steps taken to reach the big goal.

Again though, this is all in retrospect as at the time of setting this big goal, I had zero awareness of the connection of goal setting to passion and purpose. Looking back, it's clear that these deeper drivers played a major role in my success. There is incredible value in taking the time to discover and develop personal interests that may eventually blossom into something that we are truly passionate about.

What were my mini goals that lead to success? These included the development and delivery of the short presentation for the initial facilitation training, setting up the meeting with the training coordinator to pitch the larger presentation, then develop that content. Consider that mini goals should be SMART – specific, measurable, achievable, relevant, and time-based. The SMART goal concept has been utilized in different fields since 1981. Although not full-proof and applicable to every situation (Bjerke & Renger 2017), this is a valuable approach for goal setting. My initial introduction to the SMART goal concept was in 2009 while attaining my health coaching certification. The SMART concept negates vagueness in goal setting as there is a specific task, with a specific amount of work that will be completed by a specific date or timeframe. This holds the goal setter accountable. An example of a SMART mini goal for exercise is the following: on Monday, Thursday, and Saturday of every week, at 7:30am, I will resistance train for 10 minutes. This is different from "I will exercise three times a week." Through successful completion of several mini goals, one is likely to gain momentum and motivation from the small wins on their path to reaching the big goal.

SMART criteria application for health behavior change has been supported by research (Bailey 2019), and I've seen it work in real life application through my health coaching practice. I've also used it in the past to reach a big goal. In 2022, one of my big goals was to present at five conferences. Prior to that year, I only presented at one conference – ever. Being an inexperienced conference speaker who was not in demand required some legwork to find and apply for conferences, which was all done with the use of SMART mini goals. These included researching local conferences for proposal submission deadlines and ensuring that my topic fit within the framework of each conference. I tracked everything in writing. Next came submitting the proposals within specific timeframes. I also connected with individuals who were chairs in associations that held conferences that year to better the chance of my proposal's acceptance. Through this structured process, I succeeded in my big goal of presenting at the five conferences, one of which was at the national level. What did I present on at four of the five conferences? Motivation and purpose – topics that I became passionate about a year prior, hence the big goal was once again support by my intrinsic drivers.

There is no requirement to use SMART mini goals, one can achieve big goals without them – such as writing this book. Due to a very scattered schedule, I did not utilize the SMART goal process to write the book but setting the big goal at the beginning of the year, supported by passion and purpose, was adequate motivation to keep moving forward. With SMART goals I would likely have finished writing it sooner.

More On the Power of Passion

If we are passionate about what we do and possess a deeper purpose for our actions, meaning what we are passionate about also benefits others, the sky is the limit for our impact and accomplishments. A great example of this is the story of a French teenager who happened into a dentist office in 1968 due to several painful cavities. While in the waiting room, he stumbled upon a news clipping about new construction in America – the World Trade Center. He fervently read the article several times, enthralled by the two sky-touching twin buildings which would be erected in a few years in New York City. His captivation led to an early exit from the dentist's office, without getting the cavities filled, but with the article in hand and the grandeur thoughts of connecting and walking on a wire in between the roofs of these massive structures. This man was the great wire-walker Philippe Petit, and this moment was the spark that led to him accomplishing the impossible (Petit 2002).

After relocating to the United States, Phillipe illegally entered the Twin Towers countless times over the span of several years to plan and prepare for his unthinkable wire walking performance, with the last of these break-ins being Wednesday, August 7th, 1974. On the morning of that day, after a full night of rigging the wire across the towers, with the help of a few accomplices but without sleep, food, and water, Phillipe stepped foot onto the wire, just as the doors to the roof top opened and workers spilled out to start their day. Soon many police officers and other authority figures joined the workers and began pleading with the performer to abandon his daring act. Eventually the pleading turned into threats and after eight passes across the wire which lasted 45 minutes, Philippe stepped onto the South Tower and was immediately arrested (Petit 2002). In the years following this incredibly daring wire walk, he's continued to perform on the wire, has written several books, lectured at universities, and starred in an Academy Award winning documentary, among other accomplishments.

I had the pleasure of interviewing Philippe in 2019. Prior to the interview, he practiced on the wire, something that he'd been doing three hours every day for the past 55 years. During the interview, Philippe shared the following regarding goals and passion:

> *"The notion of nothing is impossible is the story of my life. (speaking to the world trade center wire walk) It's impossible, fine I know that, so let's work on it – then it's one step at a time. Without the dream as a goal, you would not be able to go one step at a time to make your dream come true. Limits exist only in people who are not dreaming, people who do not have a goal and a passion. But if you have a goal and a passion then the world becomes limitless – of course you have to be tenacious, have to have patience, you have to work on it day and night, but I think you should live your life in a way that shows limits do not exist."*

Where does passion come from and how can we garner its powers to accomplish amazing things? It starts with being interested in something and learning more about it. Consider the following questions: what do you like to do outside of your daily responsibilities? What topics or activities get you excited? What are you willing to invest your time in without any compensation? What are you willing to read a book about during your free time? What activities bring you pleasure? Too often, when I ask people these questions, I get little to nothing in response.

Considering that only 20 percent of American workers are passionate about their jobs (Schroeder 2023), there is value in finding and cultivating something that we can sink our teeth into, something that makes us feel alive, outside of the workplace. Otherwise, irrelevant of our level of perceived success, we may end up just going through the motions throughout our lifetime, with a deep void inside and regret towards the end of our time on earth.

Developing passion is not easy and finding something we are initially interested in that we can eventually become passionate about takes effort. It's much easier to come home from work, eat dinner, and plop down on the couch to decompress with a device in hand, television on, or both. Yet the easy way out is seldom a path of growth, accomplishment, or personal progression. If you currently have an interest and have not fully engaged in the process of learning more about it, start now. When you find that thing or things that captivate you, momentum will build, and you may eventually throw yourself fully and completely into your interest. Any goals set within the framework of this process will be that much easier to accomplish due to your intrinsic motivation and engagement.

Extrinsic Movers

While intrinsic motivators such as purpose and passion are ideal drivers for goal accomplishment and all our goals align with a bigger picture, sometimes an extrinsic push can help as well. An extrinsic motivator is a reward, with some of the most popular extrinsic drivers being money, sex, and fame aka being a rock star - or simply rewarding yourself for a job well done with a nice, healthy post work dinner. Overall, rewards can be impactful, but one must be mindful of their application so as not to erode intrinsic drive. Furthermore, a study of weight loss and financial incentives demonstrated initial success with weight loss but substantial regain of weight at the three-month follow-up (Volpp 2008). Getting paid to lose weight was motivating during the few months of the study but once the payments stopped, so did the motivation.

There is a fascinating reversal option to the reward angle and motivation. In his voluminous book, *The 4-Hour Chef*, Tim Ferriss pointed out the importance of accountability and incentives (rewards) for goal achievement. Interestingly, the loss of something is more motivating than the gain of the same exact thing. Hence, loss aversion can be utilized as a motivator for goal accomplishment. Ferriss recommended the website StickK.com, or a similar commitment site where individuals can put their "money where their mouth is." To up the ante even further, if one does not accomplish their goal, the money they put up will go to their favorite anti-charity. Imagine that! If you don't succeed, your hard-earned cash goes to some organization you completely despise. That would certainly motivate me.

Another successful method for goal achievement is an accountability buddy. If you are unable to identify one in your immediate family or friend circle, there are websites for this as well. This option also provides the opportunity to connect with like-minded individuals who are on a similar goal path. The business of personal coaching, whether it be life coaching, career coaching, or health coaching, has become a success due to the accountability factor involved. Someone is there, in your corner, supporting your growth, but also challenging you if you do not follow through with agreed upon progressions. One can be the most purpose driven person on the planet but can still benefit from others' support. Being both a health coach and a personal trainer at different points in my life, I've seen firsthand the motivation and eventual success that accountability can create.

Goal Setting in the Judicial System

The concept of goal setting is not reserved for personal growth only, it's been utilized for success attainment across numerous populations. Consider the judicial system, specifically individuals who are placed on probation in lieu of incarceration. Probation is supervision in the community of an individual who has committed a crime, with an effort towards rehabilitation. Keeping offenders in the community on probation supervision, while incorporating an evidence-based risk-needs-responsivity model, can lead to successful outcomes. A risk tool, which involves a structured interview to assess an offender's likelihood to commit future crimes, is used at the beginning of community supervision. If the individual is assessed as high risk, they receive the highest level of interventions to address possible future criminality before it comes to fruition. This high level of intervention requires a case plan, which is driven by goal setting and completion.

Like the model laid out by Kotler, minus purpose, offenders work with their supervising officers to develop high, hard (or big) goals. Afterwards, objectives are established (the mini goals), to move the offender towards the overarching big goal. Consider this example: an offender has a high risk for substance abuse and with the support of their probation officer, develops the big goal of obtaining/maintaining sobriety. Next, objectives or mini goals are developed to begin the process of moving towards the bigger goal. These may include a substance abuse evaluation, providing clean drug screens, attending NA/AA meetings, or enrollment in an outpatient treatment facility. Success with these objectives hopefully leads to the big goal of sobriety. The probation officer serves as the accountability holder, supporting the offender's progress, but also wielding a level of say as to the ultimate loss aversion, that being freedom if the offender violates their probation. Ideally, incarceration is avoided. During this partnership and through the process of working towards the big goal, the offender may even develop a deeper purpose. For someone overcoming substance abuse, this may be becoming a NA/AA sponsor or motivational speaker for others struggling with drug use.

Goal Setting for Health

Working with health coaching clients for years provided me with an appreciation for how impactful goal setting for health-enhancing behaviors can be. During the initial meeting with new clients, we would take an hour or two and map out their entire day, from the moment they woke to the moment they went to bed. We notated what they ate and drank throughout the day, hours spent commuting, at work, at home, any existing self-care, post-work behaviors and how work affected them, stressors, and anything else that was important and impactful. We also discussed what their overarching goal, the big goal was, and why they hired me. Once we had the big goal and a map of their average day, with the focus being on Monday to Friday as those tend to be more structured, we would determine where small changes could be implemented into the existing schedule – changes that would not require an extensive effort. The recommendations that followed would all be manageable and guided by the client. Each recommendation would be transformed into a SMART mini goal, with specific times, items, and amounts. For example, if the client wanted to incorporate exercise or movement into their life, we would figure out what day, the ideal time of the day, and the most realistic exercise for them in that timeframe. Said mini goal would look something like this: on Monday, Wednesday, and Friday at 7:00am, I will take a 15-minute walk outdoors, perform 20 push-ups, and plank for one minute. The next meeting, we discussed whether the incorporation of the new behavior was successful or not, the reality of continuing this behavior, and if things didn't go as planned, determined why. Reflection and accountability were essential to this process.

Everyone does not have the financial resources to afford a health coach, although I'm a firm believer that if everyone did, a lot of health issues could be prevented and mitigated, specifically related to lifestyle diseases such as diabetes, cancer, and heart disease. Considering a health coach is there to support the individual in incorporating lifestyle changes and behaviors geared towards enhancement of health and self-care, any long-term successes from this process would not only impact the client positively, but likely their loved ones too. Yet even without a health coach, creating a SMART and impactful health plan for oneself is a great step in the right direction. This must begin with a big goal for the betterment of one's health and wellness. Write the goal down, make it real, and ensure the piece of paper is accessible and visible. Next, assess your average day and chart what happens hour by hour, from when you wake up to when you go to sleep. After this, decide which self-care technique you want to incorporate first – is it more movement, exercise, meditation, home cooking, a healthy smoothie, intermittent fasting, or some other shift in food? Next, what part of the day is it easiest to incorporate this technique which enhances the likelihood of it becoming a long-term behavior. Now, you've chosen the technique, on these days, and at these times for this long – great, now give it a try for a month. Write this down as a SMART mini goal and implement it. After the month is over, assess whether this new behavior is sustainable. Maybe you've already experienced some benefits, which usually begins with feeling a bit better and having more energy. This should boost motivation to continue the new behavior. It'll be your decision whether you want to incorporate another behavior next or continue with the initial one until it becomes a habit. At the end of the day, self-care is a multifaceted process dependent on the level of wellness you want to achieve. If you want to be at your best or close to it every single day, you'll likely need to incorporate more than one form of self-care.

Should Weight Loss Be a Goal?

Weight loss is a challenging journey for many, with short-term success often overshadowed by long-term difficulties. A 2001 meta-analysis by Anderson et al. assessing long-term weight loss maintenance revealed that by five years, 80 percent of the lost weight was regained. The barriers to successful weight loss are substantial. This starts with the already discussed obesogenic environment in which food companies intentionally stock grocery store shelves with food-like substances designed to be addictive. Food scientists have expertly combined sugar, fat, and salt, creating the" bliss point", that ensures consumers overindulge in their employers' products. Billions of dollars are invested in advertising to hook both adults and children on processed junk food. Said food is typically high in sugar and refined carbohydrates, which are known contributors to weight gain.

The human body loves the carbs and sugar. It is not aware that several generations ago, sugar was not available in such profound quantities. All it knows is that it must attain and store as much of it as possible for the upcoming winter famine, if we consider the evolutionary perspective – a famine that of course never happens because processed food is available year-round. Hence the food system has purposely triggered the body's natural propensity for sweet stuff, which factors into the difficulty of long-term weight loss.

Attempting to lose weight using the calorie-reduction diet, which is the path most dieters take, provides further barriers. For most, after the initial few months of successful weight loss, the body begins to conspire against further progress. The combination of enhanced appetite and slowed metabolism may not only halt but can also reverse the initial success. Interestingly, the increased appetite is a stronger factor in long-term weight loss failure than the slowed metabolism (Hall & Kahan 2018).

But hey, we are human, we have willpower, and can overcome anything! Maybe willpower assists the weight loss journey for a while, as one fights through hunger and resists addictive food. Yet, if the willpower battery drains as the day progresses, and one is constantly exerting significant effort, not only with weight loss, but other life challenges, the likelihood of succumbing to a pint of temptation that's at the bottom of the freezer increases. Polidori et al. (2016) masterfully summarize the reality of long-term weight loss maintenance: "The few who successfully maintain weight loss over the long term do so by heroic and vigilant efforts to maintain behavior changes in the face of increased appetite along with persistent suppression of energy expenditure in an omnipresent obesogenic environment" (p. 9).

Considering the high probability of failure and disappointment associated with long-term weight loss, why not just stop the efforts to lose weight? Imagine a piece of line paper in front of you and a pen in your hand. Now write "Big Goal" at the top and next to it, "Lose Weight." Next, draw a line through "Lose Weight" and replace it with "Gain Health." Could this shift with the bigger, over-arching goal yield better results? What if weight loss becomes a byproduct of striving for health? With an improvement in overall health as the bigger picture, the scope of strategies for this purpose may grow beyond the ones utilized solely for weight loss. During a weight loss journey, a person may become so hyper focused on losing weight that they overlook attained benefits outside of the numbers on the weight scale. If the scale results plateau, which is likely, this may lead to frustration and quitting. Another problematic aspect of the weight loss path is dieters' generally unrealistic weigh loss expectations (Foster et al. 1997).

I suggest reframing the big goal away from probable failure and towards the promotion and enhancement of health. How do we make this transition? Think of anything long-term that you'd like to accomplish for your health and wellbeing outside of weight loss. Maybe one of your other concerns is stress reduction. Considering the connection between stress and weight gain, the strategies you incorporate for the purpose of stress reduction may result in weight loss as well. With the big picture of health attainment, using a stress-reduction strategy, the mini goals may be, 1) Monday through Friday, immediately after waking, meditate for five minutes, 2) Monday through Friday, take a 15-minute walk at 10:30am during break at work, or 3) every evening, at 9:30pm, write down one thing I am grateful for from that day in a gratitude journal. If your weight gain is indeed tied to stressed induced increased long-term cortisol levels, which is not the case for everyone (van der Valk et al. 2018), successful stress-reducing strategies may include weight loss benefits. Of course, stress reduction is not as easy to measure as weight loss via a scale, with its quick and simple feedback that can be assessed daily and drive or curb motivation. Gauging stress reduction is a more difficult process and requires a deeper self-assessment, such as whether you're noticing that you have more energy, are less irritable, or less anxious. If you want to measure the effects of stress reduction strategies directly and don't mind spending money, cortisol level testing exists.

Another health gain option is targeting body composition. Fat loss may be a better predictor of health than weight loss, as general weight loss may lead to the loss of muscle. There are several affordable devices on the market which will provide you with a relatively accurate body fat measurement, including the one I used in the self-experiment outlined in the appendix of this book. Follow the instructions on the device for guidance as to the best time of the day and ideal circumstances for accuracy of measurement. If used properly, these home devises can be effective in gauging progress over time. With the goal of reducing body fat, such as "lower body fat by five percent", the mini goals will likely include resistance training, with specific exercises, on specific days, for a specific amount of time, and an adjustment in macronutrients such as an increase in protein intake (as I did in the self-experiment) to support the resistance training and reach the goal.

Another possible weight loss adjacent goal could be to fit into a specific article of clothing, whether that be something old that you used to fit into or something that you specifically buy to motivate you. Other possible goals could center around the accomplishment of a difficult physical feat, like climbing a local mountain range, being able to complete a set of or at least one pull-up or completing a lengthy walking trail. Considering the importance of sleep for overall health and its intimate connection to obesity (Beccuti & Pannain 2011), a goal may be to normalize sleep patterns. There are several technologies available to assess quality of sleep that one can use to track this goal. Steps to reach this goal would include minimizing screen time and blue light exposure hours prior to going to sleep each night, ensuring there are no lights on in the bedroom during sleep, taking a warm bath, and utilizing nightly breathing techniques, at a specific time each night, to ready the body for sleep. Aside from the examples provided, there are many other goal options that are likely to lead to success in enhancing health, with the side benefit of losing weight.

As discussed in the chapter on motivation, any behavior change must be meaningful to the individual on a deeper, personal level for long-term success. In their research on maintenance of weight loss and obesity, Hall and Kahan (2018) point out that, "helping patients shift their locus of motivation from weight loss alone to intrinsically meaningful areas, such as health improvement, can improve long term weight and behavioral outcomes." Medical professionals can prescribe quality dietary interventions, family members can plead and beg, and friends can provide advice, all of which may spark initial motivation and short-term progress but is unlikely to support long-term change. If we set the big goal of "health gain", what will the deeper, personal drivers be? Is it to look better, feel better, be more successful, confident, energetic, happy, focused, or driven? And how would a healthier version on you live life?

Goals and Effective Efficiency

What's goal setting have to do with being effectively efficient? Once there is something we identify that we want to work on or accomplish, goal setting will assist in this process, providing a focused path. Our actions will align with our big goal, and our energy and effort will have a pinpoint accuracy to it versus wonton, scattered, or convoluted attempts. With the newfound focus, we can distinguish what deserves our time and what doesn't. The goal must start somewhere though, and it may be with one of the following big questions:

- Am I satisfied with where I am right now in life, and if not, what can I do about it?

- What further positive impact could I have on my family, friends, community, and the world?

- How would I like to grow this year?

- What is something that I'm interested in and how can I invest more of my time into it?

- What can I do to improve my health?

    These questions can be used to assess our current state and provide a starting point for possible change. Once we establish where we would like to be or what we would like to do, goal setting plays an integral part in getting there. And who knows, maybe the universe will assist in the process.

Don't Play Small

Too often in life, we shortchange ourselves and play small. We allow comfort and contentment to reign supreme and fall into a pattern of unimpactful behavior. We don't question much, lose our natural inclination for curiosity, and become passive beings. Things happen to us versus us being the stimuli that makes things happen. I've been through this, it's the default, and it's easy, especially in a world designed to keep us entrenched in mediocrity. Sometimes we realize that we are stuck, but for different reasons, don't do anything about it. The end game is a lifetime of what ifs and the last few years of life covered in a cloche of regret.

If you have a plan, a dream, a passion, do not hold it off for too long. As we age and begin the process of assessing our time on this planet, attempted and failed dreams will likely sting a lot less than ones we did not act on. Ultimately, each one of us holds ourselves accountable to be active participants in our lives. Self-reflection through the difficult questions, the deeper questions, the uncomfortable questions can be the spark to light the fire for personal growth and change, with your goals serving as the logs of wood to keep the fire going. Eventually, as more and more people see the flame get larger and larger, they will come gather around, close, together, and enjoy the warmth that you've brought to this world.

Chapter 10

Meditation

A Self-Healing Journey

Even though Dr. Phillip Shinnick was not a big fan of cruises due to the usual overindulgent environment on-board, his son delighted in these excursions. On this particular cruise, while his son was having a great time in the company of the other youth on the ship, and while most of the other passengers reveled in copious amounts of food, partying, and all-day drinking, Dr. Shinnick spent his days exercising, meditating, and practicing yoga. A few days into the cruise, an opportunity presented itself to take a boat on shore to a local island. Dr. Shinnick thought this would be a nice chance to enjoy some swimming by the beach, as well as get away from the cruise ship environment, and joined the boat ride with his son. During the ride from the cruise ship to the shore, in efforts to enhance the excitement of the journey, the boat driver purposely sped head-on into large waves, creating a roller-coaster like experience for the passengers. As the driver hit each wave, the impact initially sent the boat up in the air, and then back down, front-first directly into the water. Sitting in the front row, and with each downward projection of the boat, Dr. Shinnick grew more uneasy and uncomfortable, to the point where the water seemed like a safer option. At one moment, as the boat approached another wave, Dr. Shinnick was jettisoned off it and into the water. Within seconds, the 25,000-pound boat struck him three times – in his mid-back, lower back, and right anterior ribs. Dr. Shinnick was 70 years old at the time.

Immediately on impact, Dr. Shinnick's back was fractured, along with a concussion and other injuries. He was taken back to the cruise ship and provided with the recommendation to be helicoptered to a hospital for treatment. Having extensive background in athletics as a former Olympic long jumper, in meditation, yoga, gung fu, and qi gong, and having healed numerous sports injuries on his own, he instead chose to remain on the ship and utilize the self-healing arts until the cruise concluded. Dr. Shinnick packed himself in ice and lay still for three days, practicing qi gong, an ancient Chinese healing art centered around the concept of qi, or vital energy. As he focused his meditation on the lower abdomen, he was able to mitigate the pain of the fractured back. Unfortunately, towards the end of the third day, the pain became all encompassing, bringing Dr. Shinnick to a space of profound desperation, in which he cried out for help. In that moment of hopelessness, he came to the realization that the breath would be his way out of this painful state. For the next few hours, he focused on the breath, with the pain eventually subsiding until the cruise ship returned to land and he was transported back to New York City by boat. Yet this return was just the beginning of a long and arduous healing journey.

CAT scans taken upon Dr. Shinnick's return confirmed compression and fractured spine, along with other spinal injuries. Although some spinal fractures can be treated without surgery (using a back brace for an extended amount of time to stabilize the spine), the common medical intervention for the extent of Dr. Shinnick's injury was a steel rod surgically inserted into the spine along with opiate pain medication. With opiate use, there was a possibility that the patient would become addicted to the pain medication, especially if used for an extensive amount of time. Dr. Shinnick did not want to proceed with the conventional option, and instead chose to conduct a lengthy healing experiment without the use of common medical intervention. Although a deeply personal decision, this healing journey was a selfless process as "the traumatic experience transformed into an act of love, compassion and understanding of a process that could benefit other human beings suffering from similar conditions" (Shinnick et al. 2014, p. 14). Hence, a deeper purpose existed in an otherwise difficult situation.

Aside from the significant pain and mobility issues associated with the fractured back, there were other impediments to recovery as assessed by medical professionals. These included: "lower anterior and posterior ribs not fixed on sternum and spine, organs in spasm, bulging cranium and pain in left temple, left jaw constriction, pain to left scapula, arrhythmia, fatigue from pain, constipation, digestive difficulty, agitation, anxiety, apprehension, fear (PTSD)" (Shinnick et al. 2014, p. 14). Dr. Shinnick had the benefit of an Occidental and Oriental Therapist assisting his recovery process throughout. The only manufactured drugs administered were acetaminophen twice a day for the first eight days then oxycontin once a day for thirteen days.

The healing process was multifactorial, involving significant effort and involvement from both the therapist and Dr. Shinnick, the patient. The therapist utilized Nian Li (using will and intention), external qi gong, and the Three Buddha healing technique, as well as continuous chanting of the Medicine Buddha Sadhana, to assist in the patient's recovery:

> At first, only external qi gong was applied to the spine. Shortly, it was possible to touch the fractured vertebrae without pain and move the spine. Within three months, the hips, lower and mid back released, creating a good environment for the fractured vertebrae to heal. From there on, attention was mostly needed from the mid back up to the neck and skull where tensions due to PTSD started to develop. The body continued to be treated as a whole… (Shinnick et al. 2014, p. 8)

Significant recovery occurred within three months of treatment. As the healing process progressed, other modalities were utilized by the therapist, including acupuncture. Considering the serious trauma brought on by the injury, both physical and emotional, treatment needed to be adjusted as regression occurred and new issues arose, spurred by posture, weather, noise in environment, travel, and stress. The treatment of the setbacks took significantly longer to address versus the initial recovery period, as the post traumatic symptoms of anxiety, apprehension, fear, and agitation were the most difficult to treat.

Along with the therapist's efforts, Dr. Shinnick played a major role in his recovery. Zazen meditation, which involves still sitting with an erect spine, was practiced regularly, along with qi gong. To address the most severe pain, he took hot baths (which after four months of recovery transitioned to visiting Russian/Turkish baths for two hours of heat, followed by yoga). During the initial recovery stage, sleep was very difficult, as extreme pain arose within ten minutes of falling asleep, which then required readjustment followed by another ten minutes of sleep. Considering the excruciating nights, every morning sun brought with it great joy and relief. During the day, as the ability to move increased, Dr. Shinnick utilized yoga, specifically poses that provided the opportunity to hyperextend the spine, as in the "child's pose" position. Some days, he would stay in child's pose for significant amounts of time for pain relief. Recovery was further enhanced with the practice of animal forms, which was possible with Dr. Shinnick's background in qi gong, shaolin kung fu five animal style (learned from Master Lawrence Tan), and Native American animal forms. This involved a meditative state where one takes the form of the animal, moving like the animal, which in this case involved "extending the spine and opening up the thoracic rib cage" (Shinnick et al. 2014, p. 12). The form of the snake provided great benefits, along with other animal forms.

The healing experiment concluded after a year and a half, during which time Dr. Shinnick kept detailed daily progress notes to document the recovery process. Although success was achieved in healing a significant spinal injury with a non-manufactured drug and non-surgical approach, occasional stiffness, arthritis in the hips, and mid-back pain persisted. Two important points need to be established at this time: first, this recovery process is not in alignment with the reality of today's world, the fast-paced stress of which puts great strain on any attempts to heal a significant injury over an extended amount of time. Yet, if a surgical procedure were to be utilized in this case, the totality of the recovery time may have been longer, with the possibility of never returning to a pre-injury level of functionality, along with negative side effects from, and possible addiction to opiate pain reduction medications. Second, Dr. Shinnick's extensive background in professional athletics, meditation, yoga, kung fu, and qi gong made this specific path to recovery possible. Although very few people possess this level of ability, this story exemplifies the importance of self-care. Any regular practice that strengthens both body and mind will enhance the likelihood of recovery if we are ever befallen by a significant injury or accident. Another important consideration is Dr. Shinnick's age at the time of accident. A review of the recovery statistics from hip fractures suffered by the elderly shows that one out of every five did not survive past one-year post-injury after the fracture was surgically repaired; without surgery the one-year mortality rate was 70 percent (Mundi et al. 2014).

A Quick Trip to the City

As I drove through New York City on a dreary and rainy Sunday morning with my friend and videographer Will in the passenger seat, I felt a bit uneasy knowing that at our destination I would be doing something for the first time. Having a friend in the car to talk to for the hour and a half ride was beneficial for my nerves, plus the stress-free drive was a pleasant reprieve from the usually mind-numbing experience of driving through the Big Apple. If you ever want to drive through New York City without utilizing ultra peak levels of situational awareness, I suggest a Sunday morning. As we pulled up to the building where I would conduct my first ever interview, we lucked out with a parking spot a short walk from the front door. We got out of the car and began the brief and wet stroll. As I considered the weeks of prep and research leading up to the interview, a bit of confidence mixed in with the nervousness.

Shortly after ringing the doorbell, a tall and slender man dressed in all white with a blue tie, arrived at the other side of the windowed door and let us in. After a quick elevator ride up, we dislodged our shoes and entered Dr. Shinnick's office. The first thing I noticed about this man was his free-flowing movements, that of someone much younger. Dr. Shinnick, in his mid-70s at the time, maneuvered around the room in a spry and agile fashion. The fact that I had reviewed the research paper on his recovery from the fractured back weeks prior, made his movements that much more eye-opening. Reading about something extraordinary is one thing, seeing the personification of the extraordinary was something else. During the next thirty minutes, Dr. Shinnick showed us some of his research papers and excerpts from a book he recently wrote. We talked for a bit in preparation for the interview before proceeding to set up the space where the interview would be conducted and recorded. After it was over, the three of us talked for a bit longer, with Will and I eventually bidding farewell and heading back to New Jersey, inspired by the prior few hours.

The Long Path to a Life-Changing Habit

I'm pretty sure it all started with Kung Fu Theatre, those late 80s-early 90s Saturday and Sunday afternoons of local television featuring tales of revenge, overcoming all odds, and countless training montages all wrapped up in the mysterious magic of the martial arts. My intrigue with these ancient fighting styles continued into early adulthood, culminating in the collection of over 500 kung fu films, which are all still in my possession. Over the years came the realization that along the margins of this interest and hobby lay aspects of Eastern culture that deserved further exploration, one of which was meditation. If these kung fu Shaolin monks voluntarily spent inordinate amounts of time sitting around cross-legged and still with their eyes closed, somehow channeling internal energy to become superhuman, well then there must be something worthwhile to this practice. Little did I know that I would one day interview someone who possessed these sorts of abilities.

Initial attempts at meditation began in my early 20s, with the practice of laying yoga breathing and extension of the exhalation. The laying yoga did not become habit, but extending my exhalation somewhat did, and I continued with this intermittently for years. In my mid-20s, I took an introductory qi gong course at a local community college, which led to incorporating qi gong exercises before sleep for months after. Again though, the practice did not stick. In my early 30s there was the incorporation of five-minute evening sitting meditation, which turned into the most difficult five minutes of every day. There was the weekend retreat that included group meditations, guided meditations, and bonding with others on similar exploratory paths. There was also conscious, deep breathing every morning while walking to work, ten weeks of yoga, reintegration of qi gong, attempts at lengthier but less often meditations, yet none of it stuck – until the pandemic.

Before we get to why the behavior finally stuck, let's explore why I failed to turn meditation into a habit through many attempts across twenty years. I was certain meditation was a beneficial practice because I read about it in reputable sources. While research was conducted on mindfulness practice before the 2000s, from 2006 to 2021, the number of publications grew exponentially (Baminiwatta & Solangaarachchi 2021), with results displaying the benefits of this practice. Furthermore, the spiritual aspects of meditation intrigued me since abandoning my religious upbringing in my late teens. In line with the wise kung fu theatre masters of my youth, I was also captivated by videos of real-life internal energy masters.

Personally, having struggled with anger since I can remember, I thought that meditation could provide a calming effect on my temper. I even experienced minor benefits related to this anytime my meditation efforts extended beyond a month. Yet, no matter how much I learned about it, saw and heard about others benefiting from it, and deep down knew it would benefit me as well, it wasn't enough to turn meditation into a permanent practice. In retrospect, I failed because I did not have a clear understanding of the practice, found it difficult, and the benefits were not immediate and impactful enough to warrant long-term habit development.

The pandemic was a life-altering and difficult time for millions of people around the world. Aside from the death toll, a significant mental health impact occurred due to unprecedented isolation. In the United States, the length and severity of safety-related lockdowns depended on local State government, with some States taking deeper and longer safety measures than others. As mentioned prior, New Jersey was one of those States, with a lockdown that lasted two years. This left a lot of people with a lot of free home time on their hands, which led to isolation silver linings. As my day-to-day began to normalize a couple months into the pandemic, and I could clearly identify the portions of the day when alone time existed, I made the decision to revisit meditation, with one important difference from my prior attempts to incorporate this practice long-term. In the past, I often meditated in the evening right before bed, and while that works for some, it did not for me. I found that sitting for five minutes in the evening and completely clearing my mind (more on this misconception later) was extremely difficult as the events from the day along with what was on tap for tomorrow swirled around in my head. During the pandemic, I made a commitment to meditate first thing in the morning. Every day, right after waking and using the bathroom, I set a timer for five minutes and gave meditation one more shot.

Within days, I realized that the morning was better for me and a few weeks into the practice, five minutes became a breeze, so I doubled the time to ten. Two months later, I moved up to 15 minutes. Considering that I went with lotus position sitting meditation, over time I experienced increased mobility in my hips, hence a physical benefit from the daily practice. As spring transitioned into summer, I began using the enclosed back porch of my home and found outdoor meditation more pleasant. For the remainder of the pandemic and to this very day, four years later, I wake up every morning, use the bathroom, go to the back porch, irrelevant of the season, and meditate for 12 to 20 minutes. Once I returned to a post-pandemic life, I carved out the morning time by waking up earlier. The practice became a necessary habit, and I was willing to adjust my day for it. So, why did it finally stick?

One Day While Washing the Dishes

I am the one who washes the dishes in our home of four. This is no small feat as we cook approximately 90 percent of our food and do not use paper or plastic plates and cutlery. A lot of dishes must be washed daily. We do have a dishwasher, but a dishwasher has limitations, hence a prep wash of the dishes to get the grimy stuff off is usually necessary. Sometimes the prep wash turns into a full wash. I'm not exactly sure how and when I was relegated the role of sole dishwasher, and I don't recall a mutual agreement. My wife simply does not wash the dishes and I refuse to let them pile up, so I guess we reached this point by default. She justifies this significant dish washing discrepancy by stating that whatever she does around the house offsets my awe-inspiring efforts at the kitchen sink. A determination on the validity of her justification is not a topic for this book.

During one uneventful evening of obligatory dish washing, I was triggered or annoyed by something my wife said. I was likely already on edge due to the sink full of dishes. I don't remember exactly what she said, but in that moment, something unusual happened. My go-to stimulus-thought-emotion path for this sort of situation was short-circuited. Throughout my life, when triggered by ones closest to me, I've almost always felt anger and responded in line with that feeling. Imagine a situation where another person's behavior or words illicit an emotion in you, and you respond in a less than ideal way. Whatever the reason is for the initial development and subsequent hardening of these response pathways, whether it's because we were at some point discounted, controlled, or vulnerable, some of the emotions that arise can be shame, fear, anger, dread, or despair. Sometimes the negative emotions arise due to social expectations, like when someone cuts in front of us in line at the store. Of course, the emotions do not always have to be negative, but whether good or bad, the process of stimulus-thought-emotion happens almost automatically. We may have some level of control over our response to whatever slight occurred, but if we reach the point of a negative emotion, the damage has been done. For me, the feeling of anger when triggered or annoyed has been a go-to since I can remember with my mom, and I'd smoothly transitioned this emotional pattern and response to my wife. During this dishwashing occasion, within the miniscule timeframe of the stimulus-thought-emotion pathway, I finally found the freedom not to choose anger.

Even though Steven Kotler's *The Art of the Impossible*, already introduced in the goal setting chapter, only briefly mentions mindfulness/meditation, the few pages resonated with me more than any other resource I've read on this topic. What first attracted me to meditation - the surreal, the spiritual, the awe-inspiring - was enough to build interest in but not to implement this practice as a long-term behavior. It was a deeper understanding of the mental health benefits of meditation and practical yet powerful application to everyday life that drove long-term behavior implementation. During that moment at the kitchen sink, the months of sitting in quiet solitude paid off in the ability to stop my old, go-to anger response to my wife's words – the triggering stimuli. So, what exactly happened?

Kotler uses the term "mindfulness", I prefer meditation – consider the two synonymous for our purposes here. He proposes mindfulness as a tool for the development of freedom to choose versus being stuck in old reactive response patterns. In other words, being able to tap into the very brief space between thoughts and emotions, especially thoughts that elicit negative emotions - and decide to respond differently. This is exactly what happened to me in the situation described above. How did it work? During meditation, the goal is not to attempt thought control, complete mind clearing, nor thinking of nothing – these are futile efforts, especially for beginners, as anyone who's attempt it knows. One of the reasons meditating was difficult for me during years of prior attempts was the misconception that I had to stop thinking during the timeframe I dedicated to practicing. It's difficult to successfully implement a behavior if you don't have a clear understanding of what you are doing. Instead, what I eventually began to do is observe the thoughts or "watch the show", instead of attempts at control. Eventually, months of thought observation every morning in practice led to catching and changing a thought in a real-life situation. This shift in thought negated the emotion and response.

The Formation of a New Habit

Let's review the reasons why meditation became an everyday part of my life.

- Have a clear understanding of the new behavior you are implementing – my initial efforts at meditation did not stick because I had a misconception regarding "mind-clearing" during practice. Once I understood this was not the process, the daily practice made more sense, along with the elimination of frustration.
- Find the best time for the behavior – as discussed, evenings did not work well because my mind was way too busy (plus the misconception). When I switched practicing to the morning, immediately after waking, I was more receptive to meditation. With attempts at implementation of any new behavior, the time of the day and your schedule matters.
- Attain benefits from the new behavior – once I noticed my new ability to tap into the space where I could break through old, problematic emotional response patterns, and connected that new skill to daily meditation, there was no going back. I found this to be a monumental, life-altering benefit. This was the most powerful factor in why I've continued meditating daily for the past four years.
- Determine the ideal amount of time you're willing to spend on the new behavior – after I noticed that five and ten minutes were very doable and learned that 12-to-20- minutes provided even greater benefits, I aimed for the 12-to-20-minute timeframe daily.

Motivation to Meditate

There's a big catch to reason No. 3 above – attain benefits from the new behavior. The benefits from meditation may not come fast and may not be easily noticeable. As previously mentioned, this was one of the reasons why I failed to make meditation a permanent practice several times in years past. It's likely why others have not stuck with meditation for the same reason. Revisiting Dan Millman's three selves, my Conscious Self was completely sold on meditation, which was enough to start the practice and stick with it for a bit, but not adequate for habit formation. In 2020, my Higher Self was a vague entity that I was starting to recognize, while the Basic Self had zero part in the motivation to meditate process. Considering meditation is not a pleasurable and exciting activity, can one tap into the Basic Self for a motivational boost? Dan Millman provides insight into this possibility:

> So if we want to meditate, we can focus on how it will help us be more relaxed, more fun loving, and more easygoing; on how we'll be more attractive and more effective in life, with better concentration to make more money – to have more, be more, live more! (p. 91)

I did not tap into the Basic Self when I began meditating, only after I realized the benefits did my Basic Self get on board. With meditation, the logistical process of finding the right time of day when I was completely uninterrupted and when my willpower was the strongest were the key factors that kept me going for the first few months. Once I tapped into the benefits of thought control, the realization came that this newly acquired ability would lead to me being more controlled, pleasant, and more liked by others. Plus, I liked myself more with this newfound ability.

The Breath

During my 50-minute interview with Dr. Shinnick, one common theme permeated throughout – the importance of the breath. Essential to life, something we do 20,000 times per day on average, predominantly subconsciously, the breath is an integral part of meditation. Yet, aside from using breath as an anchor during a meditative practice, something to focus on in efforts to be present in the moment, the benefits of connecting to the breath, not only during meditation but at any time and any place, are immense. From Dr. Shinnick's focus on breath to overcome extreme pain following his boating accident, to Wim Hoff's breathing exercise exploits in extreme cold temperatures, to you or me sitting still for a few minutes and performing deep breathing exercises, the power of breath spans a wide range dependent on our efforts to connect to and garner it.

James Nestor's New York Times bestseller, *Breath*, provides an in-depth look into breathing. Nestor takes the readers on a journey to understand the debilitating health-impacts of mouth breathing, as well as the benefits of nose breathing, holding the breath, less breathing, slow breathing, and specifically slow exhaling, and provides several breathing exercises for a variety of health enhancements. The take home seems common sense – breathing is extremely important, and we should make efforts to move it from the unconscious to the conscious via regular breathing techniques. Yet, it's common to either be unaware, forget, and/or not respect the reality that breath is life. Dr. Shinnick shared the impact of connecting to breath during our interview:

> *". . . you are on a line of essence, and the line of essence is nature. Every single minute of every single day we exhale and we inhale, and if you concentrate on that you're into nature and you're into the primal vitality of life itself, and when you do that, nature teaches you, it's called the Dao-yin, starts to teach you things – you don't need a master, and what I feel is we don't need a master but we have to*

practice this on a daily basis. If people focus on the breath, things will come to them naturally because we are nature and if you focus on what's natural then your true nature will show up, and it's very nice, it's very comforting."

Dr. Shinnick shared one breathing exercise with me, the Iron Ox. To perform this, one needs a japamala, or mala for short – a string of 108 beads. Holding the beads in your hand, you place one between your fingers, inhale and exhale, and move on to the next bead until you complete the entire mala and 108 breaths. Dr. Shinnick also suggested focus on the exhalation. A long exhalation, around ten seconds for beginners, provides the opportunity to empty one's lungs. The key is to get the air out of the lungs so fresh air can enter, otherwise if you are not fully emptying your lungs, you are not gaining vitality. Nestor's work provided further benefits of lengthy exhalations: "The deeper and more softly we breathe in, and the longer we exhale, the more slowly the heart beats and the calmer we become" (p. 144). I've used breathing in different ways during my daily meditations, from the breath being a focus point to extended exhalations of up to 30 seconds per, to breathing into pain spots, a chi-gung practice for addressing pain. With these few beneficial techniques, I've barely scratched the surface of how connecting to breath provides benefits on a myriad of levels.

12-To-20-Minutes a Day

I use a timer for my daily meditation to ensure that I hit within the 12-to-20-minute sweet spot. Why this specific timeframe? As little as five minutes of daily meditation can reduce stress and lower anxiety (Kotler 2021). This is a great starting point for anyone interested in addressing these issues. As Reid states in *A Complete Guide to Chi-gung*, "meditation is the most effective antidote against stress, and with prolonged practice, meditation trains the mind not to re-act to stressful situations with the fight-or-flight response, by cultivating the virtues of detachment and emotional equanimity" (p. 249). At 12-to-20 minutes, the benefits are enhanced, as Kotler points out, to include "heightened focus, optimism, resilience, and emotional control" (p. 81). Again, seeing the real-life benefits of any new behavior will greatly enhance the likelihood of continuing it. Having already experienced the emotional control benefits of the extended meditation timeframe, I had a very personal family crisis arise in the summer of 2021, the type of situation that would have caused immense mental strain in years past. Throughout the ordeal, thanks to my daily meditation practice, I was able to focus on the positives of an otherwise terrible situation and remained incredibly resilient throughout. This boosted my motivation further to continue with the practice.

Do I ever wonder about the world beyond 12-to-20 minutes? Absolutely! Am I going to extend my meditation practice beyond this timeframe anytime soon? Highly unlikely. Why would someone who is fully aware that something greater lies beyond, not take the time and make the effort to discover this next-level consciousness? Maybe even develop the otherworldly abilities of those Kung Fu Theatre masters? Dr. Shinnick summed it up very well when we spoke – "when people stay at a specific level of meditation, it probably means they like that level of existence". That's it. At this point in my life, I am perfectly fine with heightened focus, optimism, resilience, and emotional control.

Effective Efficiency with Meditation

Meditation is a non-negotiable for me but is often an overlooked pillar of health. Most tend to focus on nutrition and exercise as the main paths towards a healthy existence, both of which provide benefits for the body and mind. Yet meditation so directly impacts our mental state and takes so little time of daily adherence, it should hold an equal, if not superior, space next to exercise and nutrition. Due to several factors (or excuses) such as "I don't have time for this", "my mind won't stop racing", "what am I getting from this anyway?", and "I'm too distracted" (Shapiro & Shapiro 2024), people tend to give up on meditation too soon. And yes, sitting in silence and attempting to focus on the breath or another anchor for the present can be difficult and feel like it's not serving any purpose. Considering immediate gratification and the pleasure principle hold significant value in present society, practicing something that requires delay of benefits goes against the norm. I'm hopeful that sharing how I've benefited from a relatively brief daily meditation practice (one percent of my day) provides motivation for others – but I'm just barely scratching the surface of this life-altering activity. Dr. Shinnick's story displays how incredibly impactful meditation as a lifestyle can be.

The beginning stages of implementing meditation can be as simple as connecting to the breath – relegating a minute or two a day to take a few deep breaths, with focus on a complete exhalation. This tells your body that everything is ok, and that you are safe. Make sure to perform diaphragm breathing instead of chest breathing. To do this, place a hand on your stomach and a hand on your chest. When you breath in and out, ensure that the hand on your stomach is moving up and down, while the hand on your chest stays still. Also, breath only through your nose. Incorporating correct, deep breathing can bring forth a sense of calmness in the moment and if practiced regularly, many health benefits for the long-term (Jamil 2023).

Ideally, you plan a specific time of the day to meditate, whether that's in the morning like me, maybe mid-day to decompress, or end of day to relax prior to bedtime. Locate a specific space in your home or work that will serve as your meditation haven. Sit in silence or use a meditation app. Once you find the timeframe and space, meditate for at least five minutes. Don't get frustrated about the incessant thoughts that continuously pop up. Notice them, let them go, and return to whatever your focus point for the present is, whether that be the breath, the body, or the voice/music of your guided meditation app. Having structure with your practice will enhance the likelihood of continuing it long term. Practice daily without expectations of benefits nor rewards. Even though it may take time to attain benefits, trust that this daily investment is impacting you positively and is as worthwhile of an activity as anything you've attempted before for self-care. Also be mindful that there are countless meditation practices out there, hence experience and experiment with different types to see what works best for you.

Of all the self-care strategies I've incorporated into my life, meditation has been the most impactful. The fact that I dedicate approximately one percent of my entire day to this practice and have gained so much from it, makes it an effectively efficient endeavor. From developing the ability to break ingrained emotional reaction patterns, to building resilience in high stress situations, to enhancing daily focus while tackling work-related tasks, no other self-care strategy has come close to the positive impact of meditation. The benefits go beyond me as these personal enhancements have strengthened relationships with others, especially close family and friends. A better me in day-to-day interactions means a more positive experience for those I interact with. I've also had the opportunity to develop and facilitate conference workshops that included information about the positive impact of meditation. Through these public speaking engagements, I've hopefully built curiosity and planted seeds in the audience regarding this practice. Considering my public speaking skills and opportunities, I feel a responsibility to share information that has not only benefited me but millions of other people for a very long time.

The Conscious Dishwasher

I walk up to the sink, notice the dirty dishes, and see them for only what they are – dirty dishes. No thoughts of how they got there, who created the mess, nor who else is unwilling to wash them. I turn on the water and while connecting to the steady sound, I observe the stream hitting the top dish, trickling down to the dishes under. I grab the dish brush with my left hand, pour some dishwashing soap on it, then grab the top dish with my right, and begin to scrub it in a steady, circular motion. After finishing with the first dish, I place it in the dry rack and grab the next dirty one from the sink. I am in the moment, the champion of the present, and as Dan Millman termed in *The Warrior Athlete*, I am the "movement master in daily life" (p. 160). When I wash dishes, I am only washing dishes; my mind is a washcloth. Have I reached this level of presence and come to complete terms with my role as the sole dishwasher in my home? No, I have not. There are great days when I am fully present while I wash, good days when I am at peace with it all, and not so good days when the sink is full, and the frustration of a perceived injustice boils over. This is my process with more good days on the horizon, as I come to terms with the reality that my wife does her part keeping our home clean. If all else fails, the paper plates and plastic forks are at the shopping market only five minutes away.

Meditation is an essential element of the effectively efficient toolkit. As mentioned, just five to six minutes a day will begin to mitigate stress and anxiety. Up your practice to 12-to-20-minutes and the benefits increase significantly. These two ranges and up to 30 minutes a day I would deem to be the limit for the goal of efficiency. Yet I absolutely support anyone willing to go beyond that timeframe. I shared Dr. Shinnick's story of recovery to demonstrate the power of this practice when incorporated into life beyond a short, set schedule. Also, I focused on benefits within the realm of health and wellness, yet meditation can serve as a gateway to a greater spiritual awakening that deserves further exploration.

Efforts to be in the present moment should not only be relegated to the planned meditation practice, but for anytime during the day. Meditation can be sitting, standing, walking, or laying. At any moment, you can connect to the present via breath, a physical activity, or something you are observing. Being in nature also provides a wonderful opportunity for connection. With the obliteration of our senses by technology, specifically smart phones, moments of complete presence are becoming rarer. Yet these moments hold so much value and enhancement for life. They provide us an occasion for curiosity, wander, and awe. And remember, the second you pull out your cellphone to capture the moment, as nice as it is to have that photo, you are no longer fully present. As famous Buddhist monk Thich Nhat Hanh said, "nothing is more precious than being in the present moment. Fully alive, fully aware."

Chapter 11

Conclusion

We Only Get One Body

Irrelevant of our respective religious and spiritual belief systems, there's no way around the reality that at this very moment, you, me, and everyone else on this planet, are here in their current body for one lifetime only. It is the vehicle for navigating our time on this planet. From the moment when we enter this world, most of us kicking and screaming, to the moment we take our last breath, the day-to-day decisions we make directly impact our life journeys. A lot of the decisions we make directly impact our bodies as well. Unfortunately, not everyone shares the same freedoms when it comes to decisions about their life and health. I hope that you are one of the lucky individuals who can make these decisions every day as there are many who do not possess this option. Having the freedom to choose how to take care of our bodies, when and what to eat, among other similar choices, puts us in a place of privilege.

The good thing about our bodies is that they are amazingly resilient and capable of taking a significant number of insults. If we take good care of them, they will reward us accordingly, if we don't, our bodies will provide countless signs and warnings before significant illness occurs. Even under great peril, if we make the necessary adjustments and incorporate self-care, along with whatever medical intervention is needed at that point, our bodies are likely to bounce back and recover.

Thankfully, strategies for self-care are countless. The content in this book describes only a few, with a focus on negating the amount of time it takes to enhance and maintain health. That path may resonate with some, but it will not resonate with all. Irrelevant of what path you take to feel great every single day, I hope that there was something in this book that provoked thought and reflection. If you don't incorporate HIT as your exercise strategy, don't set SMART goals, nor meditate, but something in this content sparked a completely different self-care process for you, that's a win and I wish you the absolute best on your health journey. Whatever your dreams and passions are, a healthy body and sharp mind will increase the likelihood of progression and success. The longer we maintain health, the longer we can make an impact, on small and large scales.

Do You Really Not Have Time?

The great dividing line
Between success and failure
Can be expressed in five words:
I did not have time.
Anonymous

I love this quote so much; I made space for it on a wall of my home gym/office so that it serves as a constant reminder. It was the impetus for a major mental shift I experienced a few years back. Due to this quote, I no longer say nor think that "I don't have time." Now, if someone proposes an activity, wants me to take part in a project, or makes a recommendation, instead I state the following: "I'm not motivated to do that right now." This phrase eliminates the "lack of time" response and puts sole ownership of not wanting to do something on me. This way, I hold myself accountable. When we say, "I don't have time", in that moment we take ourselves off the hook for whatever it is we don't want to do. If we really, really want to do something, will we usually create the time to do it? You know the answer to that question. I propose the complete elimination of "I don't have time." If my replacement phrase does not resonate with you, feel free to find a suitable one that works best for you and that will place ownership of not doing something squarely on your shoulders.

On the first page of this book, I laid out a hypothetical yet realistic weekday for the average, working American adult. It's indeed a busy day. Nevertheless, there are ample opportunities within the 24 hours to carve out time for self-care, specifically the self-care strategies in this book. High-intensity training is a versatile and impactful set of training principles that can be incorporated in the gym or in the home. Depending on which of these places you choose to exercise, you may only need to go to the gym once or twice a week, or institute very brief daily workouts in the home. The trade-off for the shortened workouts is discomfort during the time under load. Yet this discomfort may teach us to push beyond our perceived limits not only within the realm of physical exertion, but also within other aspects of our life. The goal: build and maintain muscle mass, a proven fountain of youth. At the end of the day, whether you incorporate HIT or another form of resistance training, you should challenge your muscles regularly in some capacity to enhance the likelihood of extending your health span.

High-intensity training is also very safe, which is important as we age. The last thing anyone wants after building the motivation to exercise is an injury during a workout. HIT is an excellent system for the aging population, has been used for rehabilitative purposes, and is proven to build muscle and strength. Remember, when you perform HIT, you are using the weight to stimulate the muscles, not the muscles to move the weight.

Nutrition is of paramount importance as well, and you don't have to spend excessive time in the kitchen to cook healthy meals. Whether it's a complete-meal-shake, omelet, stir fry, salad, or whatever you come up with, quality homemade meals comprised of vegetables, healthy fats, and protein can be prepped and cooked in minutes. Fasting will shorten the prep and cook time farther, with 12 hours of not eating every day a good starting point. If you are aiming to lose weight, and this may not be an ideal goal as outlined already, focus wholeheartedly on your diet. Our profit-driven food system is difficult to navigate and opposing dietary recommendations cause ample confusion, but a good place to start is with whole, natural foods. Step two is the minimization of processed foods, sugar, and simple and refined carbohydrates, far from an easy task considering how plentiful these are and how good they taste. Overall, a focus on health gain instead of weight loss may be beneficial in shifting our dietary patterns in the right direction and eliciting long-term behavior change.

Meditation is necessary as well. The continued growth of this practice within Western cultures, along with a significant uptick in scientific research yielding proven benefits, are clear signs that its impactful and here to stay. Exercise and nutrition enhanced my life, meditation changed it. Through this practice, I've become a better version of myself. It is likely the most difficult of the three to incorporate long-term, yet the most rewarding.

Several Measures Are Needed

If you incorporate regular exercise only, especially if it's effective, sustainable, and does not enhance the chances of short or long-term injuries, you will certainly experience health benefits. Focusing solely on natural, whole foods or meditation will have a positive impact on your health as well. Yet, combining these self-care tools will take you to the next level, so that you can enjoy increased daily energy, focus, concentration, resilience, and ability to take on tasks and challenges with confidence. Of course you can also take ice baths, cold showers, saunas, get massages, journal, walk in nature, practice gratitude, get more sleep, spend time with loved ones, dance, laugh more, garden, or volunteer your free time for those in need. Which brings us back to the main point of this book – making the time for self-care. What activities are you motivated to carve out time for in the 24 hours allotted to you every single day? Do you want to incorporate several effectively efficient forms of self-care or struggle to make time for one laborious strategy only? Do you want to strive for and possibly reach your highest potential every single day? Whether you're aiming for greatness or simply want to be a better version of yourself, the forms of self-care outlined in this book along with goal-setting strategies, will increase the likelihood of you accomplishing anything you want. You'll spend minimal time on self-care, show up every day at your best, make the most of your time, create the best outcomes, and be your best for others – you'll be effectively efficient!

Appendix

The Self Experiment

Disclaimer: *I have never been a proponent for any specific diet, even after this experiment. My thoughts on eating, (and I've been generally successful health-wise with this mindset), is to focus on the actual food itself, ensuring that what I consume is in its natural state, or close to it. Other than the few days towards the end of this experiment, I don't count calories or macros, and have never weighed food, although I do see the value in having awareness of these factors. When reviewing the results of this experiment, aspects such as my genetics, self-care, and anything I did not or could not control for, need to be taken into consideration. This dietary experiment was guided by my curiosity and is not a health recommendation for others.*

Question – Can I, an adult male in his mid-40s, decrease body fat through simple dietary interventions, specifically a decrease in daily carbohydrate intake and re-introduction of meat and poultry into my diet?

Hypothesis – Due to the decrease in the daily consumption of carbohydrates and increase in protein intake, a decrease in body fat may occur. Silver et al. (1993, p. 211) concluded that body fat percentage "does not appear to increase significantly after the age of 40 years," with increase in body fat appearing to be connected to weight gain. Furthermore, a systematic review and meta-analysis concluded that when older adults consumed high protein diets, they retained more lean mass and lost more fat mass (Kim et al. 2016).

Start Date and experiment timeframe: April 1st, 2023; 113 days.

Measurements for progress assessment – weight, body fat, and waist circumference.

- Starting weight: 157.1 pounds
- Starting body fat percentage: 11.4 percent
- Starting waist circumference: 30 inches

Measurement timeframes – first thing in the morning after waking and urinating.

Measurement devices

- Weight: Etekcity Scale
- Body fat percentage: Omron HBF-360C Fat Loss Monitor (handheld device)
- Waist circumference: Tape

Measuring Body Fat

Utilizing guidance from Timothy Ferris' book, *The 4-Hour Body*, I initially aimed to measure my body fat by attempting to drink one and a half liters (50 fluid ounces) of water immediately after waking. Following the water consumption, the goal was to wait 30 minutes, urinate, and measure. Mr. Ferris has conducted significant health-related experimentation on himself over the years and is a respected voice in the health industry. Unfortunately, I found consumption of that much water in the morning in that short amount of time excruciating and couldn't consume the full recommended amount. My morning usually involved comfortably sipping through 16-20 ounces of water in approximately one hour, hence this deluge of 50 ounces was out of the norm. Feeling unmotivated to go through this hyper-hydrating process every time I had to measure body fat over the next three to four months, I pivoted to measuring first thing in the morning, immediately after urinating, minus the water. This measurement timeframe is also recommended in the user's manual of the Omron HBF-306C Fat Loss Monitor.

Omron HBF-306c Fat Loss Monitor

Page three of the Fat Loss Monitor product manual states that this device will "display your estimated value of body fat percentage." The Omron HBF-30GC and other bioelectrical impedance devices have been tested in research studies against X-ray absorptiometry (DXA) and the BodPod, both considered more reliable for measuring body fat. Fahs et al. (2020) found that bioelectrical impedance devices underestimated body fat percentage, while Cruz Rivera et al. (2022, p. 4) concluded that the Omron HBF-306C "demonstrated excellent intra- and inter-device reproducibility and a strong positive correlation with body fat measures obtained from DXA scan." For my purposes, this device held value because I was the only one using it, over time, and at the same time for every measurement. Irrelevant of whether the initial measurement overestimated or underestimated my starting body fat percentage, the device gauged personal progress through consistent measurements, under the same circumstances. I aimed to take several measurements over the next three to four months to attain a decent sample size.

More on My Starting Weight and Body Fat Percentage

My starting weight was 157.1lbs, which sits on the low end for men who are 5'10 and 3/4th inches in height. My starting body fat of 11.4 percent was on the low end of normal for men between the ages of 40-59. My waist circumference of 30 inches was considered small for a man. I provide this information to display that I am a thin and fit individual already. There was minimal room for continued body fat loss, weight loss, and inches off the waist. Also, I was not attempting to lose weight through this experiment. Any weight loss was a byproduct of the fat loss goal and dietary interventions.

Controls

- Exercising – HIT training six times a week, five to six minutes time under load (TUL) each day. Every third week, HIIT on stationary bike totaling six minutes (30 seconds slow, 30-second sprint, two minutes slow, 30-second sprint, two minutes slow, 30-seconds sprint).

    (Although this is a control, it's important to point out that physical activity and exercise "have been shown to attenuate age-related decreases in muscle mass, strength, and regenerative capacity" (DiStefano & Goodpaster 2018, p. 1)).

- Intermittent Fasting (or Time-Restricted Eating) – 14-16 hours fast each day, skipping breakfast. Black coffee every morning.

- Home cooking – same home-cooked meal patterns as before, with majority of weekly meals being prepped at home. (For years, I've consumed a plant-based pescatarian diet; vegetables will be incorporated in every meal). Meal prep/cooking no more than 15-20 minutes per meal.

- Meditating - 12-20 minutes per day.

- Food quality – A predominantly natural, organic diet – the quality of the food will remain the same.

Dietary Changes

- Daily intake of beef, chicken, or fish, small to medium portion size (not weighed exactly, average four to eight ounces). This was the first time I consumed meat/poultry in 13 years.

- Daily intake of 25 grams of grass-fed whey protein isolate and five grams of creatine via 18-to-20-ounce shake. The shake also contained sources of fat, specifically walnuts and avocado. The carbohydrate was banana.

- Reduction, roughly 50 to 60 percent, in refined and simple carbohydrates, such as pasta, bread products, white rice, potatoes, carb-heavy processed foods, and sugar.

- All labeled foods I deemed dessert would not eclipse 10 grams of sugar per serving size, except for special celebratory occasions.

Additional Discussion About Dietary Changes

More on creatine – Based on prior experience with creatine use, which I've cycled on and off for several years, I expected to gain five pounds of weight. Some research supports an increase in total body weight through creatine supplementation (Kutz & Gunter 2003).

More on sugar intake – Due to expected celebrations, cook-outs, birthdays, and other outings during the timeframe of the experiment, I did not aim to eliminate sugar and carb-heavy processed foods completely. Because sugar elimination is difficult and I did not want to be "that person" at celebratory events, the mindful reduction of simple and refined carbohydrates seemed more practical, as well as the 10-gram cap on regularly consumed desserts.

Incongruent Health Tools

Sometimes when different tools for health enhancement are incorporated, the dynamics of one may get in the way of another. The first incongruency was with the incorporation of whey protein shakes. The consensus is to consume this supplement immediately following a workout for optimal benefits, specifically if one resistance trains. This timeframe, which can be as long as sixty minutes post-workout, is called the "anabolic window." I usually exercised between 6:50am and 7:00am each day followed by a fast till between 12:00pm and 1:00pm.

Therefore, I exercised on an empty stomach and maintained that empty stomach till lunch. Due to this schedule, I was not taking advantage of the "anabolic window." Despite this, I liked my schedule, and was happy with my muscle mass and strength at the beginning of the experiment. Also, research suggests that "morning is the most efficient time of day to reduce body fat through exercise, particularly since blood sugar levels are at their lowest" (Kim et al. 2015, p. 1931). Furthermore, exercise in a fasting state has been associated with an increase in human growth hormone (Dabbak 2024).

Taking these factors into consideration, I maintained my daily exercise schedule and fasting, and incorporated the shake later in the day. Half of the week, the shake was the first meal of the day post-fasting, the other half, I consumed it in the late afternoon/early evening. Even though not ideal for regeneration following a high-intensity workout, the shake still increased my daily intake of protein. Also, there is evidence that consumption of at least 30g of protein for breakfast provides muscle health benefits (Hawley & Baum 2019). Maybe the mechanism behind these benefits extends to the first meal of the day, irrelevant of what time it's consumed.

The second incongruency came with creatine consumption. The recommended time to consume creatine is right before or after the workout. I drank black coffee in the morning to assist my fasting because it curbed my appetite. Considering black coffee may blunt the performance-enhancing impact of creatine, I needed to make a choice between the two. Since I chose fasting over the protein shake, I followed suit and stuck with the coffee because the creatine was conveniently partnered with whey protein in the same shake. In the past, I have not used a creatine loading phase, which I also did not this time around. (Post-experiment reading about the effects of coffee on creatine yielded research results that coffee may not blunt the impact of creatine after all (Trexler et al. 2016)).

Outside of the 25-gram whey protein and five-gram creatine shake, which just happened to conveniently be the scoop sizes for each supplement, I scanned food labels for sugar content only. I did not count calories, count macros, weigh food, or measure anything else – until curiosity kicked in towards the end of the experiment.

To Meat or Not to Meat

As stated earlier, I had not eaten meat or poultry in approximately 13 years. In my early 30s, I began a two-step process of eliminating meat and poultry from my diet. Step one was ending beef and pork consumption. Up to that point I always enjoyed a good porkchop or steak. In fact, I was raised on delicious home-made porkchops, one of my mother's specialties. Yet eliminating these foods from my diet was rather easy. I continued to consume chicken and turkey for a few more months until something clicked, and I decided that I was done with chicken as well. A week later I realized that since I stopped eating chicken, I would have to eliminate turkey, along with all other flying, feathered creatures, from my diet.

Why did I stop eating meat and poultry? There were three specific reasons. Reason one was environmental – I opted out of meat-eating due to the environmental impact of the meat industry. It's no secret that the raising of livestock requires a significant amount of water, land, and fossil fuel (Campbell 2013). The need for this land directly contributes to deforestation. Furthermore, livestock is generally raised on an unnatural diet of soy and grain which creates the unnatural monoculture farming to feed these animals. This way of farming generally requires higher usage of pesticides and causes soil degradation, high water usage, and a decrease in biodiversity. Another major concern is the methane gas released by cows and its impact on global warming. Overall, "overwhelming evidence shows that overconsumption of meat is bad for human and environmental health…" (Rust et al. 2020, p. 1).

The second reason was the way that livestock and poultry are raised and fed. Just like any other business, growing cows and chickens for the purpose of human consumption is profit driven. The faster cows and chickens mature, using the cheapest feed, the bigger the profit. Hence the use of subsidized foods such as soy and grain for the feed, and the use of growth hormones and antibiotics to enhance the maturation rate of the animal and to keep it alive in otherwise unlivable environments. The health impact of these substances within the conventional meat available in supermarkets has been debated, yet this entire process was something that I preferred to opt out of.

The third reason was the mistreatment of the animals. I was not an animal activist, nor did I consider myself an animal lover. At the same time, I could not be part of a system that requires significant animal cruelty and suffering so that I could have beef or chicken with my rice or potatoes. Considering these three reasons, the re-introduction of conventional meat and poultry into my diet for the purpose of this experiment was out of the question. The only way I was going to eat these animals again was if they were raised locally, humanely, while eating their natural diet.

Finding the Meat and Poultry That I Was Willing to Eat

For this experiment I returned to eating meat. Finding what I was willing to eat was not easy. My first three stops resulted in failure and included Wholefoods, a farm where animals are butchered on site (which reconfirmed my reasons for not eating meat in the first place), and a local butcher. Meat and poultry at Wholefoods have an "Animal Welfare Certified" label through the Global Animal Partnership, ranging from one to five+ but lacked the highest score of five+ at the Wholefoods I visited. This score is the top tier animal welfare certification, verifying that the animal has spent their entire life on a farm. My visit to the farm where animals were butchered on site was traumatizing, especially the visual of countless hens in a cage, body to body, with literally no space to move. This was not what I was looking for. Lastly, the local butcher shop I visited, which was there since the 1930s, sourced their meat and poultry from all around the country.

Finally, a couple weeks into my search, I located a farm in nearby Pennsylvania which had exactly eight frozen New York strips remaining from a cow that was raised humanely on this farm, on its natural diet. I purchased all of them. I now had enough meat to last approximately two weeks, although this search pushed back the meat-eating portion of my experiment to April 23rd. All other dietary changes were implemented on April 1st as planned.

First Time Eating Meat in 13 Years

In line with effectively efficient cooking, I pan-seared the New York strip steak – three minutes on each side with an extra five minutes on low heat for medium-well – a total cooking time of 11 minutes. I used a highly recommended iron skillet, and ghee instead of vegetable oil. After cooking and removing the steak from the skillet, I left it on the countertop for another 10 minutes. Lastly, I plated it with a side of brussels sprouts and located a private space in my house to eat.

I had no qualms regarding what was about to happen as I had come to terms with my decision a month prior. I cut into the steak and placed the first piece in my mouth. Considering I had not experienced this in over a decade, my first thought was how chewy the meat was. A NY strip is not the most tender of cuts anyways. Taste-wise, I didn't like it or dislike it. I respected and appreciated what was happening, which was a feeling I hadn't experienced as a regular meat-eater. Around the fourth or fifth bite, I realized that I did a pretty good job of cooking this steak. The outer layer of the steak had that nice, flavorful crust with a juicy afterbite on the first couple chews. I also remembered how much I hate meat fat and did my best to cut around it. To avoid possible aftereffects tied to digestion, I consumed only half of the steak, around four ounces.

I expected little to no difference in how I felt physically after eating the steak, even though it was so long since my body processed beef. There was no immediate impact, but as time passed, I felt a bit weighed down. Eventually, the gas came, and a lot of it. The brussels sprouts could have been a confounding variable when it came to the excessive gas. My wife was negatively impacted. I realized quickly she was no longer a fan of my self-experimentation. But I knew I had to push forward.

Before sharing more, I want to recognize that my process of searching for and finding high quality meat was a privilege. Too many people do not currently, and may never, have much choice or say in what they eat as their food experience is guided by day-to-day survival and/or lack of resources. I'm extremely blessed to be able to have a choice regarding what I eat, be able to supply quality food for my family, and share this experience with you. I've worked in urban areas, specifically with underprivileged youth whose food buying experience was a walk to the local corner bodega where the only goal was to attain the most for the least amount of money. Too many inner cities have food deserts which lead to poor health outcomes for the population there. I've seen some progress in the city where I worked and lived for many years as local farms have connected with the community to set up small farmer's markets in certain sections of the city. This is a step in the right direction but there is certainly a long way to go before underprivileged populations have regular and easy access to nutritious and affordable food.

First In-Experiment Measurements

On May 1st, I had eaten steak for eight days straight and implemented all other dietary changes for one month. This felt like a good time to take measurements. The results were as follows:

- Weight: 158.3 pounds
- Body fat Percentage: 11.3 percent
- Waist circumference: 30 inches

I expected more weight gain due to the use of creatine alone but that did not occur. Everything else stayed the same.

Enter the Chicken

After eating eight NY strips over a span of two and a half weeks, prepped in all sorts of ways, I realized that I didn't need steak in my life. If these were eight of the most mouth-watering filet mignons would my mindset have been different? I don't know, maybe. It was an experience to try steak again, but not one that compelled me to keep it in my diet beyond the experiment. It's important to mention that through the process of reintroducing meat into my diet, I didn't experience any major discomfort or gastrointestinal issues, aside from the first day gaseous turbulence.

Prior to running out of steaks, with the help of my friend Dave, I was able to locate a local farm with organically and ethically raised pastured and free-range poultry. When I arrived at Wildflower Farm, I was happy to see the animals on spacious, green pastures as advertised on the farm's website. This was exactly what I was looking for. I made two separate visits and both times the owners were kind with their time as we discussed the chickens, other animals they raise, and most importantly, how to cook the four-pound birds I purchased considering how long it's been since I ate chicken. One of the recommendations I received was to season and roast the chicken as is, which sounded effectively efficient to me! The chickens, along with a few fish dishes, lasted me the next two weeks.

Second In-Experiement Measurements

A few days ago, I noticed physical changes in the mirror – I looked more defined overall, but especially in the abdomen. I didn't want to take any measurements until June 1st but felt compelled to do so on May 21st considering the perceived changes. The results were as follows:

- Weight: 155.1 pounds
- Body fat percentage: 9.9 percent
- Waist circumference: 28.5 inches

The mirror did not lie. My waist circumference was down one and a half inches from the original measurement, and body fat one and a half percent. My weight was down two pounds. I'd been eating high quality meat for four weeks, a combination of grass-fed beef, wild caught fish, and pasture-raised chicken, and had incorporated the other dietary changes for seven weeks.

I lost a couple pounds which were likely fat considering the lowering of body fat percentage. Of interest was the fact that all my prior experience with consistent creatine intake resulted in weight gain. Why the fat loss? The reintroduction of daily meat/poultry plus the whey protein led to an overall increase of protein in my diet. Furthermore, an increase in fat consumption (which I'll discuss later) combined with the conscious decrease in simple and refined carbohydrates, likely shifted my macronutrient ratios. This was worth a deeper dive.

Transition to Fish

I transitioned to solely eating wild caught fish for 10 days as the main source of protein, specifically salmon and sardines. There were three days where I reverted to a vegetarian diet as I had no quality meat/poultry/fish readily available. I continued with all other aspects of my dietary gameplan. The 10 grams of sugar max on foods deemed dessert transformed the post-meal treat into 85% dark chocolate, Trader Joes almond, cashew, and dark chocolate trail mix, yogurt, or sunflower butter cups.

Third In-Experiment Measurements

On June 2nd, the measurement results were as follows:

- Weight: 154.2 pounds
- Body fat percentage: 9.6% body fat
- Waist circumference: 28.2 inches

Considering my starting weight, body fat, and waist circumference were already on the slim side of the bell curve, I deemed these changes significant.

My assumed creatine-driven weight gain still had not materialized, but instead I lost a total 2.9 pounds. Per a review of creatine by the Cleveland Clinic, it was possible to gain two to four pounds of muscle mass while taking creatine during a four-to-12-week training cycle. Whether creatine causes water retention was up for debate, with conflicting research displaying water retention in the short-term but not over longer periods of time (Antonio 2021). Further research pointed to creatine lowering body fat when combined with resistance training in adults 50 years of age and up (Candow 2023). Whatever combination of dynamics were in play here, factoring in resistance exercise as well, my overall body composition changed. Most relevant is the fact that my body fat decreased.

There was the obvious increase in protein in my diet that likely shifted my macronutrient ratios, as already mentioned. Since eliminating meat and poultry from my diet 13 years ago, and due to my plant-based, pescetarian diet that was low in dairy as well, I may not have taken in adequate amounts of protein for years. Through this experiment, I consumed an amount of quality protein that was appropriate for the type of high-intensity resistance training that I performed. The ideal amount of protein for someone who resistance trains regularly is debatable. The general recommendation for a man my weight is 82 to 136 grams of protein daily, and some experts recommend consuming protein at a rate of body weight in grams. Yesterday, I consumed around 82 to 90 grams, at the lower end of the recommendation. This is likely more than I consumed for years before the experiment, yet still nowhere close to the body- weight-in-grams option. Regarding fat intake, even though avocado, nuts, and seeds were always staples in my diet, I increased the daily consumption of each. Nut consumption alone had averaged between 27 grams and 40 grams during the experiment, which is at and above the daily recommended amount. Recent research has shown that the human body may not digest tree nuts and peanuts well, specifically the fat content of nuts (Nikodijevic 2023). This may be why consuming nuts regularly is not associated with weight gain. Also of importance is the fact that fat and protein consumption increase satiety.

My Birthday

On June 5th I turned 45 years old. I held a small party at my home to celebrate during which time, I indulged in cake and alcoholic drinks. I then ate ice cream the next day and more left-over cake, plus celebrated with others and ate cupcakes the day after that – and drank some more. All of that was ok. Sometimes we may hyperfocus on our health, specifically our diets, and become unnecessarily rigid to the point where we stop enjoying ourselves during times when it's necessary to. A celebration weekend of drinking and enjoying cake and treats is ok – it's wonderful actually.

Fourth In-Experiment Measurements

July 1st marked three months of the experiment. I stayed regimented with the dietary program throughout, aside from my birthday and a couple other celebrations. I decided to extend the experiment three more weeks. Today's measurements were similar to the ones from June 2nd:

- Weight: 154.2 pounds
- Body fat percentage: 9.8 percent
- Waist circumference: 28.2 inches

Maybe I plateaued. Yet, I was happy with being under 10 percent body fat at 45 years old. I hadn't been under this percentage for a few years and chalked that up to the natural decrease in muscle mass as we age. Brief, continuous resistance training and a dietary shift proved otherwise.

Curiosity Peaks Its Lovely Head

"I have no special talent. I am only passionately curious."
Albert Einstein

During the past few years, I learned the importance of maintaining curiosity. If Einstein put so much value on being inquisitive, open-minded, and open to new things, there must be something to this. Considering that a likely shift in macronutrients led to my results, it was time to collect data and do something that I was totally against – counting calories and macros. I always attained health-related success focusing on food instead of numbers. Curiosity trumped my dietary belief system. Since I ate the same way and similar foods daily for the past three-plus months, I chose a sample size of three consecutive days and stayed the course with my experimental diet. Below are the results:

Three Day Average:

- Calories – 2,609 per day. This was within the range of the recommended daily amount for men per the current U.S. dietary guidelines, although trending towards the higher end.

- Daily macronutrient ratios – 38 percent fat, 34 percent carbohydrate, 28 percent protein.

My first question was whether these macro ratios were what a body builder would consume when cutting weight before a show. A bit of internet digging and cross-referencing of several on-line articles (Norton; Obadike, 2021; Abelsson 2022) provided me adequate information that a body builder's macro levels have less fat and more protein/carbs. Next, I performed a search for the term "even split diet" which led me to the Zone Diet, that utilizes a 40-30-30 carb, fat, and protein ratio. Developed by Dr. Barry Sears, the Zone Diet has been around since the 1990s. Ultimately, this seemed to be a calorie-restriction diet due to its recommendation of 1500 calories per day for men. The macros and specific food suggestions were reasonable, but of course the total calorie recommendation was not, especially if we take into consideration the reality of the body eventually pushing back on this decrease in energy consumption via an increase in hunger. Further digging led me to a book by Dr. Al Sears that I've had for years, *P.A.C.E: The 12-Minute Fitness Revolution*. I read the book twice before, yet this third time I focused specifically on the dietary information.

Per a pie chart in Sears' book, a pre-agricultural diet consisted, on average, of 31 percent protein, 38 percent fat, and 31 percent carbs, ratios eerily similar to my experimental macros. These ratios are representative of a hunter-gatherer diet. I did not necessarily follow the guidelines of what to eat within the hunter-gatherer diet recommendations, but I hit the macros. Of further interest is Sears stating that counting calories to burn fat is a myth as the human body is too complex to be considered a calorie-in versus calorie-out machine. Sears' second myth bust is that eating fat makes one fat.

The 2020-2025 Dietary Guidelines for Americans provide us with wide ranges for macronutrient recommendations, with the main concern being the carbohydrates, at anywhere between 45 percent to 65 percent of daily calories. Dr. Sears, and my personal experience, would say that this is not ideal if you aim to lose body fat, which instead would require an increase in fat and protein consumption. Of course, the quality of fat matters greatly. All the fat recommended by Sears and that I consumed were of the natural variety. The standard American diet unfortunately steers consumers towards more problematic sources of fat, such as vegetable and hydrogenated oils, which are found in a lot of processed foods. Bottom line: you may decrease body fat by shifting your macros towards quality sources of protein and fat, and away from the carbohydrates.

Sears also recommended creatine use in his book and provided research examples of how creatine supports muscle growth and athletic performance. Sears tapped into other important health-related factors which tend to be overlooked, specifically the importance of heart rate variability and lung size, both predictors of health and longevity. Heart rate variability can be increased via high-intensity interval training and any other generally challenging physical undertaking. Sears also tapped into the importance of nitric oxide, a molecule that influences many important factors such as weight, immune function, mood, and sexual function. While Sears recommends supplementing l-arginine to increase nitric oxide, in his New York Times best seller *Breath*, James Nestor recommends nose breathing to do the same.

A point of interest regarding sweets and dessert: on day three of counting, I consumed one double serving of soft serve ice cream which shifted the macro percentages in favor of carbohydrates. This serving once or twice a week may be negligible in the long run, yet the addition of a nightly indulgence is likely to have a negative impact if one aims to stay within the macro ranges that I consumed over the past few months for the purpose of decreasing body fat. If I ate ice cream nightly for the next few months, would that undo the fat loss I've experience? I'll pass on that experiment and leave it for someone else's curious mind.

All of this begs the following question: can one lose body fat and weight while consuming a diet that is close to an even split in macros with fat being the highest? Based on the way I ate for the past three months, the answer is yes. Of course, this micronutrient profile may not yield the same results for others. The 2020-2025 Dietary Guidelines for Americans recommended a wide daily fat intake range of 20 percent to 35 percent of total calories. Based on my results, someone who's macros are at 20 percent fat per day is likely to have different results if they are aiming to lose body fat versus someone who consumes 35 percent daily fat. The increase in protein intake likely also factored into my outcome. Based on the results of this experiment, steady fat and weight loss may occur through regular high-intensity training, and the daily consumption of appropriate amount of high-quality protein, natural sources of fat at the highest government recommendation and slightly above, and carbohydrates below the governmental recommendation.

Final In-Experiment Measurement

On July 22nd, I took the final measurement for this experiment:

- **Starting Measurements on April 1st, 2023**
  - Weight: 157.1 pounds
  - Body fat percentage: 11.4 percent
  - Waist circumference: 30 inches
- **Final Measurements on July 22nd, 2023 (113 days later)**
  - Weight: 154.0 pounds
  - Body fat percentage: 9.5 percent
  - Waist circumference: 28 inches

While losing 3.1 pounds of weight is not earth-shattering, decreasing body fat by two percent and two inches off my waist in three months and three weeks is impactful, especially since I started out on the slim side of the bell curve. Interestingly, around two months into this process the above numbers shifted and held steady for another seven weeks. Is it possible for me to lose more body fat and shift the composition of my body further? Yes. Am I motivated to do so? No. The process likely entails applying a bodybuilder style dietary intervention, which would require eating at very specific times and specific foods before and after workouts, with a more detailed process of measuring and weighting the food, being mindful of water intake, etc. That would not be and effectively efficient process. The interventions I applied to attain the results from this experiment did not take any extra time. Adding the easy-to-make and clean-up-after shake may have saved time as it replaced a meal that required longer prep and clean up.

The Blood Work

On August 1st, I was welcomed by my nurse practitioner into the private room at the doctor's office for my yearly physical. As I made my way to the examination area, I noticed my lab work results ready for review. I excitedly grabbed the report and began reading the first page. Before I share those results with you, it's important to share results from past bloodwork for comparison:

2019 – Predominantly plant-based/sparingly pescetarian diet – age 41
    Total cholesterol: 186
    HDL: 78
    LDL: 93
    Triglycerides: 64
    Cholesterol/HDLC Ratio: 2.4
    Non-HDL cholesterol: 108
    Fasting Glucose: 82
    Hemoglobin A1c: 5.1

2022 – Predominately plant-based/sparingly pescetarian diet – age 44
    Total cholesterol: 201
    HDL: 94
    LDL: 93
    Triglycerides: 56
    Cholesterol/HDLC Ratio: 2.1
    Non-HDL cholesterol: 107
    Fasting Glucose: 82
    Hemoglobin A1c: 5.2

August 1st, 2023 – Current experimental diet – age 45
    Total cholesterol: 228
    HDL: 89
    LDL: 127
    Triglycerides: 39
    Cholesterol/HDLC Ratio: 2.6
    Non-HDL Cholesterol: 139

Fasting Glucose: 89
Hemoglobin A1c: 5.1

Before I dive into the diet-induced differences between the recent bloodwork and the numbers from the prior year, let's quickly review bloodwork from 2019 for some context as to how my numbers have looked for most of my 30s and 40s. My diet at that time was plant-based with occasional fish intake. All the cholesterol and fat-related bloodwork falls within the "heart healthy" range. The fasting glucose and hemoglobin are within healthy ranges as well.

In 2022, the cholesterol rose to 201 but this was due to a rise in HDL only, as LDL stayed exactly the same. The triglycerides fell while the fasting glucose maintained within the healthy range, along with the hemoglobin. Next, let's review my measurements at the end of the experiment, the controls, and experimental diet one final time:

Measurements

- Age: 45
- Weight: 154 pounds
- Height: 5'10" 3/4 inches
- Body fat percentage: 9.5 percent
- Waist circumference: 28 inches

Controls

- Exercise: HIT and HIIT, six days a week – 30 to 35 minutes total TUL per week
- Food: predominantly natural, organic, home-cooked
- Meditation: 12-20 minutes per day
- Intermittent fasting: 14-16 hours daily

Experimental Diet which shifted macros in favor of fat/protein

- Re-introduction of grass-fed beef, pasture-raised chicken, plus increase in wild caught fish intake – which led to an increase in daily protein intake.

- Consumption of daily grass-fed whey protein and creatine shakes – which also led to an increase in daily protein intake.

- Consumption of fats such as avocados, nuts, sunflower seeds, dark chocolate, ghee, and grass-fed butter – which led to an increase in daily fat intake.

- Decrease in simple and refined carbohydrates – which led to a decrease in daily carbohydrate intake.

2023 Bloodwork

There was a marked increase in my overall cholesterol, from 201 to 228, into what is deemed an "at-risk" range. This was predominantly due to an increase in LDL cholesterol from 93mg/dl to 127mg/dl, with HDL dropping from 94mg/dl to 89mg/dl, although still in the high range. Interestingly, triglycerides dropped from 56mg/dl to 39mg/dl. Results from a 2024 meta-analysis provide a probable explanation for the mechanism behind these number shifts:

> The Lipid Energy Model provides a mechanistic explanation for the inverse relationship between BMI and LDL cholesterol change and the existence of the LMHR (lean mass hyper responder) phenotype, involving the greater reliance on fat for metabolic fuel. According to this model, depletion of hepatic glycogen stores with carbohydrate restriction increases adipocyte lipolysis and resynthesis of triglycerides in the liver, which are exported in VLDL particles. Increased

hepatic VLDL secretion, together with faster peripheral turnover of VLDL at adipose and lean tissues, yields a lipid profile characterized by low triglycerides, high HDL cholesterol, and high LDL cholesterol (Soto-Mota et al. 2024, p. 745).

I may fit the proposed lean mass hyper-responder (LMHR) phenotype. The important word here is "may." The general lipid profile of a LMHR includes LDL cholesterol > 200mg/dl, HDL cholesterol > 80mg/dl, and triglycerides < 70mg/dl while on a carbohydrate restrictive or ketogenic diet. The diet in my experiment was not ketogenic, but more in the range of moderate restrictive (26 percent to 45 percent of daily food comprised of carbohydrates). Although my HDL cholesterol and triglycerides were within the ranges of a LMHR, my LDL was not. If I restricted carbohydrates significantly would my LDL rise to above 200mg/dl? Maybe. The only way to find out is if I went full blown keto, which I have no plans of doing. There is also the probability of LDL cholesterol variability among individuals' response to a carbohydrate restrictive diet. Interestingly, when placed on carbohydrate restrictive diets, individuals with high BMI tend to have different cholesterol results. The meta-analysis continues,

> Whereas lean individuals experience marked elevation of LDL cholesterol, those with high BMI typically experience no change or a reduction in LDL cholesterol. Furthermore, the importance of BMI in explaining response heterogeneity appeared much greater than saturated fat. Our findings are consistent with recent data from others and contradict conventional thinking that elevations in LDL cholesterol on an LCD, when they do occur, are primarily driven by increased saturated fat intake (Soto-Mota et al. 2024, p. 743).

Further research on this topic states that, "atherogenic dyslipidemia (including high triglycerides and low HDL cholesterol) may contribute more to atherosclerotic cardiovascular disease" (Norwitz et al., 2021, p. 7). Bottom line: even though the carbohydrate-lowering dietary changes I instituted may have increased my LDL and overall cholesterol, I may also fit into a specific phenotype for whom this seems to be the norm under such a diet, and who possess adequate protective factors against heart health issues.

Final Analysis

From April 1st to July 22nd, a total of 113 days, I conducted a dietary experiment.

Through the reintroduction of meat, poultry, and grass-fed whey protein shakes into my diet, along with the increase of fish consumption, combined with a conscious lowering of simple and refined carbohydrates, I shifted my macronutrient profile. The new profile closely resembled an even distribution of fat, carbohydrate, and protein, with fat slightly above carbohydrate, which was slightly above protein. Daily fat intake ranged between the high end of the US dietary guideline recommendations (35 percent) and above. Daily carbohydrate intake was below the US dietary guideline recommendations (45 percent to 65 percent), although far from the ranges for a ketogenic diet (five percent to 10 percent). Daily protein intake was likely within the lower end of the range for someone who performs resistance exercise regularly.

Meat, poultry, and fish were not regularly introduced into the diet until the fourth week of the experiment. The first marked changes in measurements occurred one month after the full diet implementation, with lowering of weight, body fat percentage, and waist circumference. Soon after, the changes plateaued at around three pounds of weight loss, two percent decrease in body fat, and two inches of waist circumference loss. These changes maintained to the end of the experiment. Even though the results were in alignment with the hypothesis, fat loss may not have been solely due to the increase in protein intake.

A daily creatine supplement was introduced into the diet as well, at the five gram per day recommended amount, without a loading phase. Considering that past use of creatine always led to weight gain, it is interesting that I experienced weight loss during the experiment. At no point did I make any effort to decrease the amount of food nor calories consumed, and based on a small sample size, my calorie intake was within the range of the recommended daily amount for men in my age range. Unfortunately, I did not gather a sample size of daily caloric intake before the experiment, therefore there is no data for comparison to truly see if I ate less during the three months and three weeks. Also of importance is the reality that fat and protein consumption cause satiety.

As with any case study, genetics likely factored into the outcome. Already being on the lean and low body fat end of the bell curve, I instituted dietary changes that lessened the amount of carbohydrates available, which may have depleted glycogen stores (that may have already been low if indeed I fall into the LMHR phenotype), and led to the mobilization of more fat, and ultimately the difference in body fat percentage.

Most pertinent to the general population is that my shift in macronutrients was not extreme. Often, "diets" require major changes in eating, whether that is a decrease in overall caloric intake or a macronutrient shift, such as a ketogenic diet, or even a total elimination of sugar. Here, the shift was marginal across macros, which may be more practical for the purpose of long-term maintenance. Below would be the macronutrient recommendation in percentages, based on this experiment, which differs from the US dietary recommendations, yet not drastically:

Daily fat intake: 35 percent to 40 percent

Daily carbohydrate intake: 30 percent to 35 percent

Daily protein intake: 25 percent to 30 percent

In line with my goal for this experiment, a focus on losing fat instead of losing weight worked well. The shift in macronutrients, combined with resistance training through HIT, may positively alter body composition via fat loss and muscle gain. The quality of the food should also be considered. I was lucky to have the resources to access quality meat, poultry, and fish during the experiment, as well as organic food. This matters, yet what likely held more value was the decrease in simple and refined carbohydrates, and processed food. If this is simply a macronutrient math problem, then benefits should still occur if conventional foods are consumed.

Shifting Back to Real Food

This experiment started with dietary changes involving real food with the final analysis transforming the food into macronutrient percentages. Let's reverse engineer back to the foods that started this process as any shifts in diet should begin with what we are putting in our mouths, not numbers or percentages. As outlined already, my daily diet consisted of one high quality protein in the form of meat, poultry, or fish, small to medium portion size, a 25-gram whey protein shake with five grams of creatine, natural forms of fat which included nuts, seeds, avocado, ghee, grass-fed butter, as well as plenty of vegetables. I also ate eggs regularly, which were already a steady part of my diet, and the occasional low carb protein bar. I minimized consumption of pasta, bread, rice, carb-heavy processed foods, and sugar, and occasionally replaced these with complex carbohydrates. I ate fruit as well, mostly berries.

You may be wondering what this looked like in daily meals? Below is an example:

Fast until 12pm to 1pm, 12-to-16-ounce black coffee and water.

First meal: 18-to-20-ounce shake consisting of whey protein, creatine, avocado, banana, strawberries, coconut milk, and ice.

Second meal: two-egg omelet with zucchini, mushrooms, sunflower seeds, peppers, bean sprouts, cooked on ghee, with a slice of buttered sourdough bread.

Third meal: one smoked whiting or baked salmon with capers and walnuts, plus side of vegetable mix (broccoli, cauliflower, carrots, etc.)

Snacks: cottage cheese or yogurt, and trail mix (almonds, cashews, dark chocolate)

A Few Months Later and Into 2024

I continued to eat in alignment with the experimental diet and maintained low bodyfat into the Fall. On October 2nd, I took the following measurements:

Weight: 152.2 pounds

Body fat percentage: 8.9 percent

Waist circumference: 28 inches

As the days got shorter and colder, I slowly reverted to the same diet I've maintained for the 13 years prior to the experiment, a plant-based/pescatarian way of eating. I no longer focused on ensuring that I consumed a daily quality protein, and I cycled off the creatine. I also stopped consuming whey protein in my shakes, instead opting for a vegan protein powder. I was not as consistent with the shakes either. Even though I maintained all prior controlled self-care variables, that being high-intensity training, meditation, home cooking, and predominantly high-quality food, my weight, body fat percentage, and waist circumference reverted to pre-experiment numbers.

References

Abelsson, A. (2022). Macros for cutting: Count your way to fat loss. *Strengthlog. com*. https://www.strengthlog.com/macros-for-cutting/

Adult activity: An overview. (2023, December 20). Center for Disease Control and Prevention. https://www.cdc.gov/physical-activity-basics/guidelines/adults.html

Alnawwar, M. A., Alraddadi, M. I., Algethmi, R. A., Salem, G. A., Salem, M. A., & Alharbi, A. A. (2023). The Effect of Physical Activity on Sleep Quality and Sleep Disorder: A Systematic Review. *Cureus*, *15*(8), e43595. https://doi.org/10.7759/cureus.43595

American time use survey – 2023 results. (2024, Jule 27). Bureau of Labor Statistics, U.S. Department of Labor. https://www.bls.gov/news.release/pdf/atus.pdf

Anderson, J. W., Konz, E. C., Frederich, R. C., & Wood, C. L. (2001). Long-term weight-loss maintenance: a meta-analysis of US studies. *The American journal of clinical nutrition*, *74*(5), 579–584. https://doi.org/10.1093/ajcn/74.5.579

Anton, S. D., Moehl, K., Donahoo, W. T., Marosi, K., Lee, S. A., Mainous, A. G., 3rd, Leeuwenburgh, C., & Mattson, M. P. (2018). Flipping the Metabolic Switch: Understanding and Applying the Health Benefits of Fasting. *Obesity (Silver Spring, Md.)*, *26*(2), 254–268. https://doi.org/10.1002/oby.22065

Antonio, J., Candow, D.G., Forbes, S.C., Gualano, B., Jagim, A.R., Kreider, R.B., Rawson, E.S., Smith-Ryan, A.E., VanDusseldorp, T.A., Willoughby, D.S., Ziegenfuss, T.N. (2021). Common questions and misconceptions about creatine supplementation: What does the scientific evidence really show? *Journal of the International Society of Sports Nutrition*, 18, article number 13. https://doi.org/10.1186/s12970-021-00412-w

Asprey, D. (2014). *The bulletproof diet: Lose up to a pound a day, reclaim energy and focus, upgrade your life.* New York: Rodale.

Attia, P. (2023). *Outlive: The science & art of longevity.* New York: Harmony.

Axe, J. (2016). *Eat dirt: Why leaky gut may be the cause of your health problems and 5 surprising steps to cure it.* New York: Harper Wave.

Backlund, B., & Miller, R. (2015). *Backlund: From all-American boy to professional wrestling's world champion.* New York: Sports Publishing.

Bailey R. R. (2017). Goal Setting and Action Planning for Health Behavior Change. *American journal of lifestyle medicine*, *13*(6), 615–618. https://doi.org/10.1177/1559827617729634

Barber, T. M., Kabisch, S., Pfeiffer, A. F. H., & Weickert, M. O. (2020). The Health Benefits of Dietary Fibre. *Nutrients*, *12*(10), 3209. https://doi.org/10.3390/nu12103209

Barrell, A. (2023, June 9). What happens to the body after sitting down for too long? *Medical News Today*. https://www.medicalnewstoday.com/articles/sitting-down-all-day#:~:text=Physical%20activity%20is%20a%20crucial,day%20sitting%20down%2C%20on%20average.

Baye, D. (1998, April 26). High-intensity strength training for cardiovascular conditioning and fat loss. Baye.com. https://baye.com/high-intensity-strength-training-for-cardiovascular-conditioning-and-fat-loss/

Bernard, N. (1993). *Food for life: How the new four food groups can save your life.* New York: Crown Trade Paperbacks.

Beccuti, G., & Pannain, S. (2011). Sleep and obesity. *Current opinion in clinical nutrition and metabolic care*, *14*(4), 402–412. https://doi.org/10.1097/MCO.0b013e3283479109

Black, D. S., O'Reilly, G. A., Olmstead, R., Breen, E. C., & Irwin, M. R. (2015). Mindfulness meditation and improvement in sleep quality and daytime impairment among older adults with sleep disturbances: a randomized clinical trial. *JAMA internal medicine*, *175*(4), 494–501. https://doi.org/10.1001/jamainternmed.2014.8081

Blackburn, E., & Epel, E. (2017). *The telomere effect*. New York: Grand Central Publishing.

Bjerke, M.B., Renger, R. (2017). Being smart about writing SMART objectives. *Evaluation and Program Planning*, volume 61, 125-127. https://doi.org/10.1016/j.evalprogplan.2016.12.009

Campbell, T. C. (2013). *Whole: Rethinking the science of nutrition*. Dallas: BenBella Books, Inc.

Candow, D.G., Prokopidis, K., Forbes, S.C., Rusterholz, F., Campbell, B.I., Ostojic, S.M. (2023). Resistance exercise and creatine supplementation on fat mass in adults < 50 years of age: A systematic review and meta-analysis. Nutrients, 15(20), 1-12. https://doi.org/10.3390/nu15204343

Carpenter, G. (2024, March 6). How many people work remotely? *B2BReviews.com*. https://www.b2breviews.com/remoteworkstatistics/#:~:text=As%20of%20August%202023%2C%2012.2,prefer%20a%20hybrid%20work%20schedule.

Costa, D. (2023, October 13). *24-hour clock. Encyclopedia Britannica*. https://www.britannica.com/topic/24-hour-clock

Cox C. E. (2017). Role of Physical Activity for Weight Loss and Weight Maintenance. *Diabetes spectrum: a publication of the American Diabetes Association*, *30*(3), 157–160. https://doi.org/10.2337/ds17-0013

Creatine (2023). My.clevelandclinic.org. https://my.clevelandclinic.org/health/treatments/17674-creatine

Cruz Rivera, P. N., Goldstein, R. L., Polak, M., Lazzari, A. A., Moy, M. L., & Wan, E. S. (2022). Performance of bioelectrical impedance analysis compared to dual X-ray absorptiometry (DXA) in Veterans with COPD. *Scientific reports*, *12*(1), 1946. https://doi.org/10.1038/s41598-022-05887-4

Current, A. (2021). *Science of strength training: Understand the anatomy and physiology to transform your body.* New York: Penguin Random House.

Dabbak, J. (2024). Training on an empty stomach. Australian Institute of Fitness. https://fitness.edu.au/the-fitness-zone/training-on-an-empty-stomach/#:~:text=3-Growth%20Hormone%20Release%3A%20 Fasted,%2C%20metabolism%2C%20and%20muscle%20development.

Darden, E. (2004). *The new high-intensity training.* New York: Rodale.

Davis, W (2011). *Wheat belly: Lose the wheat, lose the weight, and find your path back to health.* New York: Rodale.

Deci, E. (1995). *Why we do what we do: Understanding self-motivation.* New York: Penguin Books.

Distefano, G., & Goodpaster, B. H. (2018). Effects of Exercise and Aging on Skeletal Muscle. *Cold Spring Harbor perspectives in medicine, 8*(3), a029785. https://doi.org/10.1101/cshperspect.a029785

Di Stefano, S. (2021). *The resistance training revolution: The no-cardio way to burn fat and age proof your body – in only 60 Minutes a Week.* New York: Hachette Books.

Does creatine make you gain weight? The research may surprise you! (2023). Takecareof.com. Medically reviewed by Dr. Carla Montrond Correia, ND, CNS. www.takecareof.com/articles/does-creatine-make-you-gain-weight.

Duckworth, A. (2016). *Grit, the power of passion and perseverance.* New York: Scribner.

Duhigg, C. (2012). *The power of habit: Why we do what we do in life and business.* New York: Random House Trade Paperbacks.

Exploring time spent on cooking, reading, and other activities for national hobby month. (2024, January 29). U.S. Bureau of Labor Statistics. https://www.bls.gov/opub/ted/2024/exploring-time-spent-on-cooking-reading-and-other-activities-for-national-hobby-month.htm.

Fahs, C., Boring, J., LeVault, L., Varner, W., Beck, M. (2020). The accuracy of commercially available upper and lower body bioelectrical impedance analyzers in men and women. *Biomedical Physics & Engineering Express*, 6(3):035017. https://doi.org/10.1088/2057-1976/ab8269.

Ferris, T. (2010). *The 4-hour body: An uncommon guide to rapid fat loss, incredible sex, and becoming superhuman.* New York: Harmony Books.

Ferriss, T. (2012*). The 4-hour chef: The simple path to cooking like a pro, learning anything, and living the good life.* Boston: Houghton Mifflin Harcourt.

Fife, B. (1999). *The coconut oil miracle.* New York: Avery.

Foster, G. D., Wadden, T. A., Vogt, R. A., & Brewer, G. (1997). What is a reasonable weight loss? Patients' expectations and evaluations of obesity treatment outcomes. *Journal of consulting and clinical psychology, 65*(1), 79–85. https://doi.org/10.1037//0022-006x.65.1.79

Fung, J (2016). *The obesity code: Unlocking the secrets of weight loss.* British Columbia: Greystone.

Fung, J., & Moore, J. (2016). *The complete guide to fasting: Heal your body through intermittent, alternate-day, and extended fasting.* Las Vegas: Victory Belt Publishing.

Fuhrman, J. (2003). *Eat to live: The amazing nutrient-rich program for fast and sustained weight loss.* New York: Little, Brown and Company.

Gibala, M. (2017). *The one-minute workout: Science shows a way to get fit that's smarter, faster, shorter.* New York: Avery.

Giessing, J., Eichmann, B., Steele, J., & Fisher, J. (2016). A comparison of low volume 'high-intensity-training' and high volume traditional resistance training methods on muscular performance, body composition, and subjective assessments of training. *Biology of sport, 33*(3), 241–249. https://doi.org/10.5604/20831862.1201813

Godos, J., Grosso, G., Castellano, S., Galvano, F., Caraci, F., & Ferri, R. (2021). Association between diet and sleep quality: A systematic review. *Sleep medicine reviews, 57*, 101430. https://doi.org/10.1016/j.smrv.2021.101430

Goodwin, E. (2023, June 21). More Americans work out at home than in gyms, citing convenience. *CivicScience.com.* https://civicscience.com/more-americans-work-out-at-home-than-in-gyms-citing-convenience/

Hall C. (2001). Imagery in sport and exercise In Singer R., Hausenblas H., & Janelle C. (Eds.), *Handbook of sport psychology* (pp. 529–549). New York, NY: Wiley.

Hall, K. D., & Kahan, S. (2018). Maintenance of Lost Weight and Long-Term Management of Obesity. *The Medical clinics of North America*, *102*(1), 183–197. https://doi.org/10.1016/j.mcna.2017.08.012

Hall, K. D., Farooqi, I. S., Friedman, J. M., Klein, S., Loos, R. J. F., Mangelsdorf, D. J., O'Rahilly, S., Ravussin, E., Redman, L. M., Ryan, D. H., Speakman, J. R., & Tobias, D. K. (2022). The energy balance model of obesity: beyond calories in, calories out. *The American journal of clinical nutrition*, *115*(5), 1243–1254. https://doi.org/10.1093/ajcn/nqac031

Hamrick, K. (2016, November 7). Americans spend an average of 37 minutes a day preparing and serving food and cleaning up. *Economic Research Service*. https://www.ers.usda.gov/amber-waves/2016/november/americans-spend-an-average-of-37-minutes-a-day-preparing-and-serving-food-and-cleaning-up/

Harris-Love, M., Gollie, J.M., & Keogh, J.W. (2021). Eccentric exercise: Adaptations and applications for health and performance. *Journal of Functional Morphology and Kinesiology*, 6(4), 1-12. https://doi.org/10.3390/jfmk6040096.

Hass, C. J., Garzarella, L., de Hoyos, D., & Pollock, M. L. (2000). Single versus multiple sets in long-term recreational weightlifters. *Medicine and science in sports and exercise*, *32*(1), 235–242. https://doi.org/10.1097/00005768-200001000-00035

Hawley, A., Baum, J.I. (2019). The benefits of 30 grams of protein at breakfast. University of Arkansas Division of Agriculture Research & Extension. https://www.uaex.uada.edu/publications/pdf/FSFCS98.pdf

Hedayatpour, N., & Falla, D. (2015). Physiological and Neural Adaptations to Eccentric Exercise: Mechanisms and Considerations for Training. *BioMed research international*, *2015*, 193741. https://doi.org/10.1155/2015/193741

How much physical activity do adults need? (2022, June 2). CDC. https://www.cdc.gov/physical-activity-basics/guidelines/adults.html#:~:text=Physical%20activity%20is%20one%20of/,muscle-strengthening%20activity%20each%20week.

How much time do US adults spend watching tv? (2023, March 31). Marketing Charts. https://www.marketingcharts.com/television/tv-audiences-and-consumption-229018

Hyman, M. (2023). *Young forever: The secrets to living your longest, healthiest life.* New York: Little, Brown Spark.

Jamil, A., Gutlapalli, S. D., Ali, M., Oble, M. J. P., Sonia, S. N., George, S., Shahi, S. R., Ali, Z., Abaza, A., & Mohammed, L. (2023). Meditation and Its Mental and Physical Health Benefits in 2023. *Cureus, 15*(6), e40650. https://doi.org/10.7759/cureus.40650

Jakubowicz, D., Barnea, M., Wainstein, J., & Froy, O. (2013). High caloric intake at breakfast vs. dinner differentially influences weight loss of overweight and obese women. *Obesity (Silver Spring, Md.), 21*(12), 2504–2512. https://doi.org/10.1002/oby.20460

Kellman, R. (2014). *The microbiome diet: The scientifically proven way to restore your gut health and achieve permanent weight loss.* Philadelphia: Da Capo Lifelong Books.

Khoury, B., Sharma, M., Rush, S. E., & Fournier, C. (2015). Mindfulness-based stress reduction for healthy individuals: A meta-analysis. *Journal of psychosomatic research, 78*(6), 519–528. https://doi.org/10.1016/j.jpsychores.2015.03.009

Kim, T. W., Lee, S. H., Choi, K. H., Kim, D. H., & Han, T. K. (2015). Comparison of the effects of acute exercise after overnight fasting and breakfast on energy substrate and hormone levels in obese men. *Journal of physical therapy science, 27*(6), 1929–1932. https://doi.org/10.1589/jpts.27.1929

Kim, J. E., O'Connor, L. E., Sands, L. P., Slebodnik, M. B., & Campbell, W. W. (2016). Effects of dietary protein intake on body composition changes after weight loss in older adults: a systematic review and meta-analysis. *Nutrition reviews, 74*(3), 210–224. https://doi.org/10.1093/nutrit/nuv065

Kline, J. B., Krauss, J. R., Maher, S. F., & Qu, X. (2013). Core strength training using a combination of home exercises and a dynamic sling system for the management of low back pain in pre-professional ballet dancers: a case series. *Journal of dance medicine & science: official publication of the International Association for Dance Medicine & Science, 17*(1), 24–33. https://doi.org/10.12678/1089-313x.17.1.24

Kotler, S. (2021). *The Art of impossible: A peak performance primer*. New York: Harper Wave.

Kutz, M. R., & Gunter, M. J. (2003). Creatine monohydrate supplementation on body weight and percent body fat. *Journal of strength and conditioning research, 17*(4), 817–821. https://doi.org/10.1519/1533-4287(2003)017<0817:cmsobw>2.0.co;2

Lam, A.G., Sterling, S., & Margines, E. (2015). Effects of five-minute mindfulness meditation on mental health care professionals. https://www.semanticscholar.org/paper/Effects-of-Five-Minute-Mindfulness-on-Lam-Sterling/7a7529a9e6401679016ab78f398eaaf4487aff84

Liu, Y., Wheaton, A. G., Chapman, D. P., Cunningham, T. J., Lu, H., & Croft, J. B. (2016). Prevalence of Healthy Sleep Duration among Adults--United States, 2014. *MMWR. Morbidity and mortality weekly report, 65*(6), 137–141. https://doi.org/10.15585/mmwr.mm6506a1

Ludwig, D. (2016). *Always hungry? Conquer cravings, retrain your fat cells & lose weight permanently*. New York: Grand Central L&S.

Mahindru, A., Patil, P., & Agrawal, V. (2023). Role of Physical Activity on Mental Health and Well-Being: A Review. *Cureus, 15*(1), e33475. https://doi.org/10.7759/cureus.33475

Marston, K.J., Newton, M.J., Brown, B.M., Rainey-Smith, S.R., Bird, S., Martins, R.N., & Peiffer, J.J. (2017). Intense resistance exercise increases peripheral brain-derived neurotrophic factor. *Journal of Science and Medicine in Sport*, 20(10), 899-903. https://doi.org/10.1016/j.jsams.2017.03.015.

Masood, B., & Moorthy, M. (2023). Causes of obesity: A review. *Clinical medicine (London, England), 23*(4), 284–291. https://doi.org/10.7861/clinmed.2023-0168

Mattson, M. P., Longo, V. D., & Harvie, M. (2017). Impact of intermittent fasting on health and disease processes. *Ageing research reviews*, *39*, 46–58. https://doi.org/10.1016/j.arr.2016.10.005

McGuff, D., & Little, J. (2009). *Body by science: A research-based program for strength training, body building, and complete fitness in 12 minutes a week.* New York: McGraw-Hill.

Millman, D. (1979). *The warrior athlete, body, mind, and spirit: Self-transformation through total training.* Walpole: Stillpoint Publishing.

Millman, D. (1992). *No ordinary moments: A peaceful warrior's guide to daily life.* Tiburon: HJ Kramer Inc.

Mishra, S., Persons, P. A., Lorenzo, A. M., Chaliki, S. S., & Bersoux, S. (2023). Time-Restricted Eating and Its Metabolic Benefits. *Journal of clinical medicine*, *12*(22), 7007. https://doi.org/10.3390/jcm12227007

Moon, J., & Koh, G. (2020). Clinical Evidence and Mechanisms of High-Protein Diet-Induced Weight Loss. *Journal of obesity & metabolic syndrome*, *29*(3), 166–173. https://doi.org/10.7570/jomes20028

Moro, T., Tinsley, G., Bianco, A., Marcolin, G., Pacelli, Q. F., Battaglia, G., Palma, A., Gentil, P., Neri, M., & Paoli, A. (2016). Effects of eight weeks of time-restricted feeding (16/8) on basal metabolism, maximal strength, body composition, inflammation, and cardiovascular risk factors in resistance-trained males. *Journal of translational medicine*, *14*(1), 290. https://doi.org/10.1186/s12967-016-1044-0

Mundi S, Pindiprolu B, Simunovic N, Bhandari M. Similar mortality rates in hip fracture patients over the past 31 years: A systematic review of RCTs. *Acta Orthopaedica*. 2014;85(1):54-9. https://doi.org/10.3109/17453674.2013.878831

Nago, E. S., Lachat, C. K., Dossa, R. A., & Kolsteren, P. W. (2014). Association of out-of-home eating with anthropometric changes: a systematic review of prospective studies. *Critical reviews in food science and nutrition*, *54*(9), 1103–1116. https://doi.org/10.1080/10408398.2011.627095

National Research Council (US); Institute of Medicine (US); Woolf SH, Aron L, editors. U.S. Health in International Perspective: Shorter Lives, Poorer Health. Washington (DC): National Academies Press (US); 2013. Summary. Available from: https://www.ncbi.nlm.nih.gov/books/NBK154469/

Neck C. P., & Manz C. C. (1992). Thought self-leadership: The influence of self-talk and mental imagery on performance. *Journal of Organizational Behavior*, , 681–699. https://doi.org/10.1002/job.4030130705

Nestle, M. (2002). Food politics: How the food industry influences nutrition and health. Berkeley: University of California Press.

Nestor, J. (2020). *Breath: The new science of a lost art*. New York: Riverhead Books.

Nikodijevic, C.J., Probst, Y.C., Tan, S., Neale, E.P. (2023). The metabolizable energy and lipid bioaccessibility of tree nuts and peanuts: A systematic review with narrative synthesis of human and in vitro studies. Advances in Nutrition, 14(4), 796-818. https://doi.org/10.1016/j.advnut.2023.03.006

Norton, L. The ultimate cutting diet – devised by pro natural bodybuilder Layne Norton. Simplyshredded.com. https://www.simplyshredded.com/layne-norton-the-most-effective-cutting-diet.html

Norwitz, N.G., Feldman, D., Soto-Mota, A., Kalayjian, T., Ludwig, D.S. (2021). Elevated LDL cholesterol with a carbohydrate-restricted diet: evidence for a "lean mass hyper-responder" phenotype. Current *Development in Nutrition*, Nov 30;6(1). http://doi.org/10.1093/cdn/nzab144

Obadike, O. (2021). What's the magical macronutrient ratio for fat loss? Bodybuilding.com. https://www.bodybuilding.com/content/ask-the-ripped-dude-magical-macronutrient-ratio-for-fat-loss.htm

Ortiz-Ospina, E., Giattino, C., & Roser, M. (2020, November). Time use. Our World in Data. https://ourworldindata.org/time-use

Perlmutter, D. (2015). *Brain maker: The power of gut microbes to heal and protect your brain – for life*. New York: Little, Brown and Company.

Petit, P. (2002). *The walk*. New York: Skyhorse Publishing.

Pollan, M. (2008). *In defense of food: An eater's manifesto*. New York: Penguin Books.

Poti, J. M., Braga, B., & Qin, B. (2017). Ultra-processed Food Intake and Obesity: What Really Matters for Health-Processing or Nutrient Content? *Current obesity reports*, 6(4), 420–431. https://doi.org/10.1007/s13679-017-0285-4

Ratey, J. (2008). *Spark: The revolutionary new science of exercise and the brain*. New York: Little, Brown Spark.

Reid, D. (1998). *A complete guide to chi-gung: Harnessing the power of the universe*. Boston: Shambhala.

Restak, R.M. (1984, July 28). The Jim Fix neurosis: running yourself to death. The Washington Post. https://www.washingtonpost.com/archive/opinions/1984/07/29/the-jim-fixx-neurosis-running-yourself-to-death/681bd977-8295-4d4a-802c-bbfd54684be5/

Rodgers, E. (2023, September 19). 75+ fast food consumption statistics. Drive Research. https://driveresearch.com/market-research-company-blog/fast-food-consumption-statistics/

Roig, M., O'Brien, K., Kirk, G., Murray, R., McKinnon, P., Shadgan, B., & Reid, W.D. (2009). The effects of eccentric versus concentric resistance training on muscle strength and mass in healthy adults: A systematic review with meta-analysis. *British Journal of Sports Medicine*, 43(8), 556-68. https://doi.org/10.1136/bjsm.2008.051417.

Ruegsegger, G. N., & Booth, F. W. (2018). Health Benefits of Exercise. *Cold Spring Harbor perspectives in medicine*, 8(7), a029694. https://doi.org/10.1101/cshperspect.a029694

Rust, N. A., Ridding, L., Ward, C., Clark, B., Kehoe, L., Dora, M., Whittingham, M. J., McGowan, P., Chaudhary, A., Reynolds, C. J., Trivedy, C., & West, N. (2020). How to transition to reduced-meat diets that benefit people and the planet. *The Science of the total environment*, 718, 137208. https://doi.org/10.1016/j.scitotenv.2020.137208

Sears, A. (2010). *P.A.C.E. The 12-minute fitness revolution*. Royal Palm Beach: Wellness Research & Consulting.

Schoenfeld, B., Contreras, B., Krieger, J., Grgic, J., Delcastillo, K., Belliard, R., & Alto, A. (2019). Resistance training volume enhances muscle hypertrophy but not strength in trained men. *Medicine & Science in Sports & Exercise*, 51(1), 94-103. https://doi.org/10.1249/MSS.0000000000001764.

Schroeder, B. (2023, Sept 14). 80% of career employees not passionate about work. Reduce your risk as you migrate to becoming an entrepreneur. *Forbes.com*. https://www.forbes.com/sites/bernhardschroeder/2023/09/14/8-of-career-employees-not-passionate-about-work-reduce-your-risk-as-you-migrate-to-becoming-an-entrepreneur/

Schwarzenegger, A. (2023). *Be useful.* New York: Penguin Press.

Shapiro, E., &, Shapiro, D. (2024, January 11). Why we find it hard to meditate. Mindful Magazine. https://www.mindful.org/why-we-find-it-hard-to-meditate/#:~:text=This%20experience%20of%20the%20mind,idea%20how%20to%20be%20still.

Shinnick, P., Porter, L., & Mandigo, C. E. The science of whole person self-healing: Global treatments for a traumatic spinal injury. ResearchGate, Vol 7 No. 25 Oct. 2014, pp. 5-17. https://www.researchgate.net/publication/267211424_The_Science_of_Whole_Person_Self-Healing_Global_Treatments_for_a_Traumtic_Spinal_Injury

Silver, A. J., Guillen, C. P., Kahl, M. J., & Morley, J. E. (1993). Effect of aging on body fat. Journal of the American Geriatrics Society, 41(3), 211–213. https://doi.org/10.1111/j.1532-5415.1993.tb06693.x

Smith, L. (2023, Jan 6). 41 exercise statistics: The latest fitness trends. The Good Body. https://www.thegoodbody.com/fitness-statistics/

Soto-Mota, A., Flores-Jurado, Y., Norwitz, N., Feldman, D., Pereira, M., Danaei, G., Ludwig, D. (2024). Increased low-density lipoprotein cholesterol on a low carbohydrate diet in adults with normal but not high body weight: A meta-analysis. *The American Journal of Clinical Nutrition*, 119(3), 740-747. https://doi.org/10.1016/j.ajcnut.2024.01.009.

Starrett, K. (2016). *Deskbound: Standing up to a sitting world.* Las Vegas: Victory Belt Publishing.

Steele, J., Fisher, J., Giessing, J., Androulakis-Korakakis, P., Wolf, M., Kroeske, B., & Reuters, R. (2021, January 27). Long-term time-course of strength adaptation to minimal dose resistance training: Retrospective longitudinal growth modelling of a large cohort through training records. https://doi.org/10.31236/osf.io/eq485

Stozer, A., Vodopivc, P., & Krizabcic Bombek, L. (2020). Pathophysiology of exercise-induced muscle damage and its structural, functional, metabolic, and clinical consequences. *Physiological Research*, 69(4), 565-598. https://doi.org/10.33549/physiolres.934371.

Taubes, G. (2007). *Good calories, bad Calories: Fats, carbs, and the controversial science of diet and health*. New York: Anchor Books.

Trexler, E., Smith-Ryan, A., Roelofs, E., Hirsch, K., Persky, A., Mock, M. (2016). Effects of coffee and caffeine anhydrous intake during creatine loading. *The Journal of Strength and Conditioning Research*, 30(5), 1438-1446. https://doi.org/10.1519/JSC.0000000000001223.

Temple N. J. (2022). The Origins of the Obesity Epidemic in the USA- Lessons for Today. *Nutrients*, *14*(20), 4253. https://doi.org/10.3390/nu14204253

United States Census Bureau. (2022). *Average travel time to work (in minutes) in United* States *is 26.4*. https://www.data.census.gov/all?q=average+commute+time

U.S. Department of Health and Human Services and U.S. Department of Agriculture. *2020-2025 Dietary Guidelines for Americans*. 9th Edition. December 2020. DietaryGuidelines.gov

U.S. Department of Health and Human Services. (2018) Physical Activity Guidelines for Americans, 2nd Edition. Retrieved from https://health.gov/paguidelines/second-edition/pdf/Physical_Activity_Guidelines_2nd_edition.pdf

Van Kessel, P. (2020, Feb 5). How Americans feel about satisfactions and stresses of modern life. *Pewresearch.org*. https://www.pewresearch.org/short-reads/2020/02/05/ how-americans-feel-about-the-satisfactions-and-stresses-of-modern-life/

Vasquez N. A., & Buehler R. (2007). Seeing future success: Does imagery perspective influence achievement motivation? *Personality and Social Psychology Bulletin*, , 1392–1405. https://doi.org/10.1177/0146167207304541

Vo, L. T. (2012, September 17). *What Americans actually do all weekend, in 2 graphics*. NPR. https://www.npr.org/sections/money/2012/09/17/161272259/what-americans-actually-do-all-weekend-in-2-graphics

Volpp, K. G., John, L. K., Troxel, A. B., Norton, L., Fassbender, J., & Loewenstein, G. (2008). Financial incentive-based approaches for weight loss: a randomized trial. *JAMA*, *300*(22), 2631–2637. https://doi.org/10.1001/jama.2008.804

Wang, Y., Liu, Z., Han, Y., Xu, J., Huang, W., & Li, Z. (2018). Medium Chain Triglycerides enhances exercise endurance through the increased mitochondrial biogenesis and metabolism. *PloS one*, *13*(2), e0191182. https://doi.org/10.1371/journal.pone.0191182

Weiler, M., Hertzler, S. R., & Dvoretskiy, S. (2023). Is It Time to Reconsider the U.S. Recommendations for Dietary Protein and Amino Acid Intake? Nutrients, 15(4), 838. https://doi.org/10.3390/nu15040838

Westwater, M. L., Fletcher, P. C., & Ziauddeen, H. (2016). Sugar addiction: the state of the science. *European journal of nutrition*, *55*(Suppl 2), 55–69. https://doi.org/10.1007/s00394-016-1229-6

Wewege, M.A., Desai, I., Honey, C. Coorie, B., Jones, M.D., Clifford, B.K., Leake, H.B., Hagstrom, A. (2021). The effects of resistance training in healthy adults on body fat percentage, fat mass and visceral fat: A systematic review and meta-analysis. *Sports Medicine*, volume 52, 287-300. https://link.springer.com/article/10.1007/s40279-021-01562-2#:~:text=Compared%20to%20the%20control%2C%20resistance,%25%20confidence%20interval%20−%200.87%20to%20−

Wilhelmi de Toledo, F., Grundler, F., Bergouignan, A., Drinda, S., & Michalsen, A. (2019). Safety, health improvement and well-being during a 4 to 21-day fasting period in an observational study including 1422 subjects. *PloS one*, *14*(1), e0209353. https://doi.org/10.1371/journal.pone.0209353

Wiley, T.S., & Fromby, B. (2000). *Lights out: Sleep, sugar, and survival.* New York: Atria Paperback.

Wu G. (2016). Dietary protein intake and human health. *Food & function, 7*(3), 1251–1265. https://doi.org/10.1039/c5fo01530h

Made in the USA
Middletown, DE
13 November 2024

64141719R10124